Donna,

Keep Meditating!

& Stay Wonderful!

xoxo

ALSO BY FARZANA JAFFER JERAJ

20 Beautiful Women Vol. 2

COMING SOON

I Cheat at Sleep

I Cheat at Confidence

I Cheat at Happiness

I Cheat at Life

I Cheat at Meditation
Zen in 60 Seconds
© 2014 by Farzana Jaffer Jeraj

First Edition

Library and Archives Canada Cataloguing in Publication

Jeraj, Farzana Jaffer, author
    I Cheat at Meditation: Zen in 60 Seconds / Farzana Jaffer Jeraj;
    foreword by Joseph McClendon III.

(I cheat at)
The supplemental audio is available for download at:
    www.icheatatmeditation.com/member.
Includes bibliographical references.
Issued in print, electronic and audio formats.

ISBN 978-0-9952059-0-1 (paperback)
eISBN 978-0-9952059-1-8 (html)
aISBN 978-0-9952059-2-5 (MP3)

    1. Zen meditations. I. Title.
BQ9265.6.J47 2016   294.3'927   C2016-904051-8
                                          C2016-904052-6

Published in Canada by Cheeky House Publishing Inc.

Printed and Bound in Canada
Book Design and jacket design by Brady Dahmer / Central Branch
Illustrations by Mo Sherwood
10 9 8 7 6 5 4 3 2 1 0

CHEEKY
HOUSE
PUBLISHING

I CHEAT
AT MEDITATION

Zen In 60 Seconds

To Papa.

The very first feminist I ever knew.

Thank you for believing in me and always

encouraging me in my work. I'm sorry I didn't finish

my book in time for you to read it.

You are missed.

GRATITUDE

Mom and Dad for supporting me through thick and thin and nurturing my inner idealist and dreamer.

My family, especially my brother, for being my sounding board.

Joseph, for your friendship and support.

Keith, for providing me with a paradise to write in.

Bethany, for your magnificent presence.

Michael S., you were the first person who read this in its roughest stages and encouraged me.

Paul, for your support and friendship.

To everyone who played editor and gave me feedback. I cherish you with gratitude: Clarissa, Sebastian & Cookie. Collin. Chris. Jay. Ish. Rozeena. Janice. Kevin. The Antonakoses. Alastair. Aaron. Kevin. Yasmin. Shazya. Alicia. Sharad. Michael. Mike. Sally. Brent. Pamela. Julia. Cracote.

Support Crew: The Guys. Marc. Sean G. Paul. Sean M. Scott. Drew. Peter. Sarah. Chris & Gillian. Jarrod. Shaleena. Brady. Nick.

To everyone else who helped after the manuscript left my hands...

Thank you. Thank you. Thank you.

TABLE OF CONTENTS

You could
lifetime
the light
down
or you can
that you
the

spend a
waiting for
to shine
upon you,
realize
were always
light.

FOREWORD

When I met Farzana, 19 years ago, it was clear even then that she was a beautiful force of nature. I have watched her grow into what I can only describe as a warm beacon of possibility and love. She is a gifted and passionate young woman and a skilled practitioner with whom I have enjoyed the benefit of sessions.

For better or worse, we live in a fast paced, gotta have it now, just add water and stir, high stressed world. Farzana's simple user friendly techniques allow anyone, with the desire, to create measurable change easily and quickly.

The "I Cheat at Meditation" technique enables even the toughest of meditation strugglers to quickly and easily create results appropriate to our time and place, our fast-paced-unto-frenetic world.

Of course, I wanted to learn how to cheat at meditation also. Her technique is outstanding and efficient. It works. I know. You as a reader are lucky to have these tools at your disposal and her voice in your home.

It is a tool that every entrepreneur and every self-actualizing individual should have in their toolkit. With this technique there are no longer any obstacles to taking up meditation.

I totally cheat at meditation too!
– Joseph McCLendon III, PhD Author of *Get Happy Now!*

INTRODUCTION

Stress has been a part of our lives dating back to the hunter gatherer days. Since then, the human race has evolved scientifically, technologically and socially. As we have evolved, so have the stressors affecting us.

Dating back to the earliest known societies and even the societies of myth, meditation has been regarded as a powerful tool in dealing with stress. Historically, many highly successful people practised some form of meditation. They used meditation to overcome obstacles as well as for personal development. They were our spiritual and religious figures. They were our heroes and warriors. They were our scientists and inventors.

The various methods of meditation evolved along with the needs of the ages and were tailored to suit the specific needs of the individual. Monks swearing vows of celibacy learned detachment-style meditations that were intended to help them curb their sexual urges. Soothsayers, shamans, priests and visionaries practised meditations that expanded the mind, allowing them to leave behind awareness of the physical world. In the Middle East, Muslim people fast for an entire month and devote themselves to their prayers. Work hours are shortened and rest is encouraged during the hottest hours of the day to accommodate the lowered energy resulting from fasting. Society accommodates the meditative practice and prayer so much so that entire cities cease their activities five times a day to engage in prayers. This is not so in most places today.

Today, most of us have not chosen an ascetic life of celibacy, nor do our work and extra-curricular schedules permit us vast amounts of time to sit in meditation. Let's face it, most of us live in a world where we are bombarded with stimuli. There are endless tasks for us to do. We have relationships to nurture, businesses to build, endless streams of red tape to filter through, less money for our time and less overall security where our basic human needs are concerned. Times have changed.

MASLOW'S HIERARCHY OF NEEDS IN THE TECHNOLOGICAL ERA

When I developed this meditation technique, I did it to accommodate the needs of our age. Most of us don't need the kinds of meditations that would assist monks in maintaining their sanity in solitude. We don't require a meditation that will help us to completely detach from our physical existence. We can't afford to be spaced out in our interactions. We have things we need to do. **We need to be sharp and alert**, but we also **want to feel calm and clear of mind** while we focus on the tasks before us. Most of all, **we need the energy** to carry out those tasks.

We have so many things that we wish to do on top of the things we have to do. Time is scarce and that is why we need something that will replenish us and give us the rest we require immediately. The technique needed to be easy to learn. It needed to be accessible at almost any moment and thus easy to incorporate into our daily life. It had to be easy to learn and even easier to practice. Most of all, it needed to be something that would get us results today and in the years to come.

AUTHOR'S NOTE

To those of you who have an advanced meditation practice and for those of you who are beginning your journey into meditation and the mind, I have intentionally oversimplified the subtleties of the mind and meditation. I felt it was important to make things easy to digest and also to allow you your own experience as you move forward in your journey.

The first rendering of this book was significantly more detailed and explored research into neuroscience and neuroplasticity. A few hundred pages long, it read a lot more like a master's thesis than a book that was intended to assist people in "cheating" at meditation. While the "neuro-stuff" is still very much a part of the process, I decided to deliver it in a format similar to what I give to my execs, athletes and clients who don't have a lot of time. Let's face it: Few of us have time to spare and what little time we do have, we have no difficulty in spending it.

You have airport security to thank for the concise delivery of this book. Had my laptop not been wiped, inadvertently, losing the entire first draft, you would not have the book that is before you today, which I believe to be much more digestible and fun. When I rewrote this material I chose to focus on the essential elements and came back to the basics because simple works. This version was written to be easy and accessible to the busy person. That's us!

My intention in writing this book was to make the blissfulness of meditation free of religion and so accessible that everyone who tries it will become forever addicted and want more. I see a world of calm, happy, kind, well-rested, clear and focused people. In other words, *Zen in 60 Seconds*.

HOW TO READ THIS BOOK

I wrote this book with the intention of giving you everything you would need to be able to learn the "I Cheat at Meditation" technique and a touch extra. I want you be able to integrate the steps, as quickly as possible, so you can use it on your own in a way that will have a lasting and powerful impact for you.

More than anything, I know how busy we all are and respect the need to have information delivered in a concise way. I wanted to deliver it so your experience would be as close as possible to us discussing it over a soothing beverage. That is ultimately my favourite way to share this process with others.

I've written every section in conversational language and I've kept the paragraphs in shortened segments for an easier read and used subheadings and lists to separate ideas. Wherever possible, I've inserted diagrams and links to resources to supplement your experience and I've laid it out so that it is easier to digest down to how the margins have been set.

The best way to read this book is from beginning to end and to listen to the audio files as they come up.

Yes, there is an audio component to the book. I know that for some, audio can be a deterrent, but I promise it will make a huge difference. This is one of those times when it's not what you do, it's how you do it. Listen to it! It is the most important part of the process. I have done my best to use illustrations to assist you in how to do the technique; however, understanding it and getting the deepest experience out of it is going to happen when you listen to the audio. If you were to only look at the images and listen to the audio files you would have the technique. That said, I'm biased so I'd prefer that you read it and experience the audio for the full benefit. Plus, I spent a lot of time writing it (twice, I might add).

Without experiencing the audio the technique won't sink in the same way. It's a whole thing about your mind and brainwaves and encoding, which I've also included a cheat sheet on in the book.

Please feel free to write in the book. <u>Underline things</u> and make notes. I won't be offended. I promise. Besides, it's your book.

You may also notice a tone of playfulness mixed in among the neuro-stuff and cartoons (illustrated by Mo Sherwood). This was also intentional. Seriously, why should young children be the only ones to have fun while learning. When we are having fun and laughing our brains are engaged in unique ways, we have an increased flow of neurotransmitters, all that "sciency" stuff, some other big words … and thus we encode new information more easily.

I also added some **cheater's tips** throughout the book and a Q&A section towards the end of the book to address the frequently asked questions.

Everything about this book was intentional from the way the content is delivered to the choice of colour and texture of the paper.

Listen to the audio (I know I've said this already, but do it! I want you to be a successful cheater.) If you skim the book to get the steps, you may not understand how to do them. The secret is in the experience. It's all about how you learn it, how you encode it, and that you practise it later in that same way.

So, be kind to yourself and have fun. Smiling is permitted and laughter is encouraged. Happy cheating!

Get your audio at **www.icheatatmeditation.com/member** and stay tuned for updates and bonuses.

Why call it cheating?

cheat \'chēt\ verb

transitive . . .

3. to elude or thwart as if by outwitting <cheat death>
intransitive . . .

3. to position oneself defensively near a particular area
in anticipation of play in that area <the shortstop was
cheating toward second base>

– Merriam-Webster Dictionary, online

cheat \'chēt\ verb

1. to strategically learn from the errors and successes
of others and employ that learning to reach one's
goals more quickly and without incident.

cheat.er\ noun

1. one who shows playful intelligence in employing
the most appropriate and efficient strategy towards
reaching their goal.

– The Farzana Dictionary of Outstanding Excellence

It's taken me 30 years of meditating to realize that it doesn't have to take 30 years to feel the benefits of it.

ALL IN GOOD FUN

Did the title, "I Cheat at Meditation" get your attention?
Did it appeal to you or did it, perhaps, offend you?

Playful cheekiness aside, it was never meant to be of disrespect to pre-existing traditions and lineages of meditation.

After a lifetime of practising and studying all kinds of meditation, I have a deep respect for the pre-existing traditions and I would not have been able to develop this process without them.

I've spent the last 30 years meditating daily. Some of it was formal, but much of it was without structure like the time spent staring at clouds on a swing set as a child or at the ceiling as a teenager. My journey in meditation led me to spend several weeks at a time in silence, study with monks, meditate with sound and gongs and to practise mantra-based meditations like transcendental meditation and Sahaj Samadi. I've enjoyed experiencing moving meditations, sweat lodge vision-quests and extended Vipasana journeys. I have been fortunate to study yoga and the enlightenment aspects of tantra as well as psychology and the mind. It has been an incredible journey.

That said, it's taken me approximately 30 years of meditating to realize that it doesn't have to take 30 years to get good at it. It certainly doesn't need to take 30 years to feel the benefits of it.

I have decided that easier is better, especially when one is starting out.

If you can learn and practise meditation in less time and receive all of the benefits, then why not?

Easy is better and this is so easy.

The reason I call it cheating is that once you have mastered this technique you will achieve deep states of meditative brainwaves in under a minute every time.

The blissfulness of meditation can be scientifically measured in brainwaves by EEG (electroencephalography). With other practices, you may or may not achieve the deepest relaxation that comes with lower brainwaves every time. We will get into brainwaves in a couple of chapters.

IN SEARCH OF PARADISE

Many people spend years meditating, endeavouring to achieve enlightenment. We want paradise. We want Shangri-La. We want to experience the light. We want Zen. We want to have that same calmness that people who meditate seem to exude. This is why we meditate.

Most people hope to see the light and expect that the light is going to miraculously shine down upon them, with a chorus of angels singing "Ahhhh."

This isn't usually the case. You could spend your entire life searching for the light in futility.

Experiencing the light is about feeling your awareness of being a part of the light. It comes the moment you realize you always were the light. Those who see the light realize they never needed to search for it. They realize they were the light all along.

The journey to this realization is a beautiful one and the process you will learn in this book is going to make this journey much easier. Once you've mastered the process, where you go with it is limited only by your imagination.

Cheater's Query

What is the light to you?

The term light in the context of meditation is one that has many religious and spiritual connotations, but it can mean anything. It could be a deeper awareness or sense of self. Perhaps it is the mastery over one's mind and body. Maybe for you it is the ability to see light, hope or possibility regardless of the challenges of your life. Maybe the light means everything to you including God, angels and aliens.

Enjoy the journey.
Stop looking.
Practice.
Do.
Let.
Allow.
Accept.
Be.

2

Cheating aside, why do we want to meditate?

paradise par·a·dise \ˈper-ə-ˌdīs\ noun

– a very beautiful, pleasant, or peaceful place
  that seems to be perfect

– a place that is perfect for a particular activity
  or for a person who enjoys that activity

– a state of complete happiness

Full definition of paradise

1 a. Eden
. . .c : Heaven

2. a place or state of bliss, felicity, or delight . . .

Synonyms

Heaven, Avalon, Elysian Fields, Utopia, Shangri-
La, Nirvana, Fanafillah, Garden of Eden, Valhalla,
transcendence.

– *Adapted from Merriam-Webster Dictionary, online*

I don't meditate for the calmness. I meditate to remember who I am.

SHANGRI-LA

Imagine a plush jungle forest. There are pathways in this forest leading to many places and somewhere in there you've heard of a paradise. Shangri-La.

The people who have been there come back forever changed. They return with incredible stories from their time there. Some people even live there and are able to come and go regularly.

You've dreamt of going, but you've heard the way is challenging. Few ever get there, for some it takes many years. Some have gotten close and caught glimpses, but have never been able to find their way back again.

Imagine living in paradise. You feel that wonderful peacefulness. When you are here you are healed in every way. In this place your worries, fears and challenges seem to dissolve away. **Here, all of the illusions which you thought were your life seem to disappear and you can finally be yourself.** Unhindered and free. You glow and you realize that it has never been about being something you're not, but being completely yourself.

Let's face it, we all want to live in this place. That's why you picked up this book.

There is a way there and it's much easier than anyone ever conceived of. Once you learn this technique you will have a fast and easy way to access the paradise within your own mind.

The reason I call it cheating is that once you have mastered this technique you will achieve deep states of meditative brainwaves in under a minute every time.

As previously mentioned, the blissfulness of meditation can be scientifically measured in brainwaves by EEG (electroencephalography). With other practices, you may or may not achieve the deepest relaxation that comes with lower brainwaves every time. We will get into brainwaves in a couple of chapters.

MY FIRST SHANGRI-LA EXPERIENCE

I was about four years old when I had my first experience with meditation. It would awaken in me what would become an obsession with the mind and its incredible potential.

The vividness of that first meditation is as clear in my mind today as it was all those years ago.

If you've ever woken up at 4 a.m. you've likely experienced that hair raising feeling on the back of your neck. It's like electricity in the air mingled with a sleepy viscosity. I awoke that morning in awe of this feeling. I had a feeling of certainty in my gut that something really important was going to happen. I also remember feeling quite grown up as my mother let me have chai for the first time (in Indian culture, your first cup of tea is a big deal). I still remember her pouring it from saucer to saucer to cool it down so we could be on our way to meditation.

As we drove to the prayer hall in silence, I could sense my mom's sleepiness, like a part of her was awake and yet some of her was still in a dream-like state. I felt quite similarly. So alert and clear of mind and yet this wonderful dreamy sleepiness continued to linger. As we drove, the world around me felt like the ocean in its calmest state. Beautiful and silky. Beneath the surface of these smooth waters, I had a sense of people dreaming deeply. It was incredible to drive through it all. When we arrived at the prayer hall, once again there was more chai.

There isn't much direction to speak of during these morning prayers, merely a dark room where you can sit with others in silence. My mom told me to take my prayer beads and recite various mantras but somehow this didn't feel right to me.

I had this sense of being part of something much greater than myself.

Something I felt I needed to listen to. That viscosity in the air was what was most real - it a part of me - and I a part of it. So…I sat…and I asked, "…what do I do?"

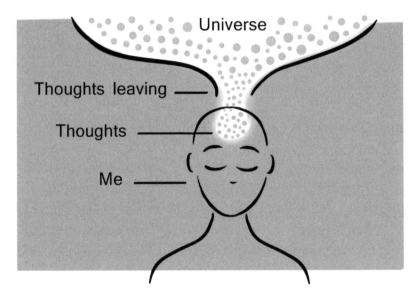

A corridor appeared in my mind, wide at its openings and narrow at its centre. My thoughts entered the corridor where they paused in the narrowest part and then released off into that greater part which I now usually refer to as the universe. As a preschooler, I didn't have that many thoughts, and very quickly I found the corridor dissolving away and myself surrounded in the most peaceful, warm silence I have ever experienced.

Though many of my beliefs around spirituality have changed; I had an awareness in that moment that I still draw from. That feeling and the things that I perceived thereafter in that first meditation affected me so profoundly that ever since I have awoken in the morning if only for 15 minutes to meditate. This started my journey of exploration into the world of meditation.

Your potential inner thoughts:
"That's never going to happen for me"
"She only experienced that because she's special. A prodigy."

Thoughts like these are the reason, I never wanted to share my story in this book.

You don't have to be have to be special, gifted or endowed by the powers that be to get the benefits of meditation. You don't have to be spiritual to meditate.

So, why did I share my story?

I decided to share it because it highlights how a child's mind is primed for successful meditation. Their minds do not have the preconceptions that meditation is hard. Thus, **a child's mind only needs exposure to meditation.**

I was fortunate enough to get that exposure and more fortunate to happen upon the Shangri-La in my mind at a very young age. This is not the norm for most people. Most people come to meditation later in life. The pathways of their brains have been moulded in very specific ways. As such, most adults tend to struggle with meditation. They must work around the existing pathways in their minds to unlearn their habits and mental patterns. They must find their inner Shangri-La and learn to enjoy it. The mind of a child is fresh and open. They don't have these limiting beliefs surrounding their ability to learn and practice meditation. Limiting beliefs are learned.

> **Experiment**
>
> Staying up all night till 4am is not the same as waking up at that time. If you havent done it before, try waking up at that time and let me know how it was for you! Don't worry, I won't judge you for falling back to sleep.

With this technique I will help you find your inner Shangri-La in a way that is simple and easy and bypasses the normal barriers we have learned.

I believe that all it takes is one good experience to get hooked. My first visit got me hooked and my hope is that by learning to cheat at meditation you will bypass the obstacles to your Shangri-La and have that one good experience that gets you hooked and coming back for more.

WHY DO I MEDITATE?

The personal reasons we seek out meditation are infinite. Before I share my answer, I feel it important to state that **there is no right or wrong answer to why anyone should meditate**. There are no "shoulds" only our subjective desires and intentions.

I believe, meditation is about much more than seeing some light that is external to ourselves. I believe it is an awareness of being part of something greater than myself. I also believe that there is science in this.

Philosophy and the meaning of life aside, Where does this fit into our daily lives?

To me it is a reminder of who I truly am in all of my potential. Me at my best. My minute and my meditation practice is a reminder of myself at the core of my being. The me that exists beyond the experiences and events of my life. The me that I could see, that we could all see in our baby pictures. That incredible potential that is still within each and every one of us. I believe, and you don't have to agree with me to make the technique work for you, that this core essence of myself may have been present before I came into this perception of my life as Farzana. I believe it will be there after I depart. It is present when I am happy. It is present when I'm in periods of stagnation. It is present when my heart is broken and I feel that all is lost. It is present when I'm feeling the gratitude and wonder of an epiphany.

It is me. It is who I am, was and always will be.

My meditation helps me to remove what I believe to be the illusions of this life. It helps me to separate the experiences of this life from who I truly am. My practice reminds me of who I really am in my core beliefs and values. It is a moment to exercise my choice over what those beliefs and values are. I use it as a reminder of the choice I always have of how I wish to experience any moment and that anything I may be going through in my life is just one small moment in my infinite life. **I don't meditate for the calmness. I meditate to remember who I am.** The calmness is a very favourable side effect.

I consider the 60 seconds to zen as my 60 seconds back to myself.

Whether meditation is a spiritual process for you or one of self-awareness and empowerment, it is still a process of training your brain to consistently access a state of bliss that is healing and resourceful. What that bliss is for you specifically is your choice.

A SUCCESSFUL CHEATER

As discussed, I meditate to remember who I am, but I have also learned that who we are is a result of what we believe.

But what makes up our beliefs? What is the difference between a belief and a thought?

While thoughts come and go, beliefs tend to be more fixed, and our value-based beliefs make up who we are. If we change our values and beliefs, we change our identity. But sometimes we entertain new thoughts and without realizing it we make them our own.

We've all heard that practice makes perfect and most of us have heard that practice makes permanent. That the more you do something, the more likely it is to become a permanent habit. We've all had that experience where we started spending time with a new person or dated someone and picked up their speech patterns. It is said that the five people you spend the most time with are the ones you will become the most like.

It goes deeper than this.

Have you ever tried on a new habit, adopted a saying, or experimented with trying on a new disposition and after a time you realized you had done it so often it had become a part of your identity? We all do this to some extent, we attach to ourselves values. We say, "I'm a laid back person" or "I'm not very forgiving". But there is also the ability to choose what we attach to our identities and what are simply things we do from time to time. Having one argument with one person or a hundred arguments with a hundred people doesn't have to make you an argumentative person. Maybe you're a litigator? (Insert laughter here or at least a little smile before we get serious again).

Nothing could be truer than a story of a woman I encountered who had extreme anxiety. When I met her, she had been hospitalized for her anxiety and was shaking and scattered. She adamantly believed that she was an anxious person. She was insistent that her mother and her grandmother were also very anxious people and she had inherited this trait. She was insistent that this was just the way it was going to be for her.

I believe that even if we have a genetic predisposition towards a temperament, that we can still practise something we would like more of. We are all mould-able. After teaching this lady how to cheat at meditation and demonstrating to her that she could feel calm it was easy to show her calmness was something she was capable of. It was something she could do. She could then train herself to feel this way more often.

It was remarkable to watch her transformation as she practised the technique again and again. Supporting her realization - that she could define who she was and be her best self through practice and choice - was and is the most fulfilling part of my work.

ACTIVITY

Take a moment to reflect on what you have attached to yourself.
Choose what you would like to attach to yourself in the future.
Practice it as often as possible everywhere you go all the time.

You are not
actions. You
of the things
happened to
a result of the
make today.
who you
choose what

your past
are not a sum
that have
you. You are
choices you
You choose
are and you
you believe.

THE PRACTICAL SIDE OF CHEATING

AKA. WHEN? HOW? WHERE?

We've talked about the abstract side of meditation. I shared what I get out of meditation and that may or may not lure you in or appeal to you. All the same, the effects of meditation are infinite and encompassing. Furthermore, the technique you're going to learn here can be used easily throughout your daily routine, to shift habits and basically bring a pleasantness to your daily life. You will be able to cheat at changing your emotional and mental states to more resourceful ones and you can also use your technique to reinforce, reprogram and process your emotions.

YOUR DAILY ROUTINES AND HABITS ARE OPPORTUNITIES FOR CHEATING

• Upon waking in the morning and at bedtime;
• In the bathroom (sitting or gazing at your good looking self);
• At the gym or while walking/running;
• While drinking a cup of coffee;

- While the children are napping;
- While the children are screaming units of destructive power;
- Standing in line or in a waiting room;
- Instead of a cigarette;
- With a glass of water;
- While on a break, and
- To stop rumination.

OCCASIONS FOR ACCESSING RESOURCEFUL EMOTIONAL STATES ARE OTHER OPPORTUNITIES

- Before a performance or a speech;
- Before a competition (even, before a golf swing);
- Before and after surgery or any other medical procedure (before giving blood);
- Before you go into work or into a meeting;
- Before you go on a date or an interview;
- Before and after opening your laptop or opening mail;
- Getting into the "work zone;"
- Accessing your creative state;
- Before studying or writing an exam, to enhance memorization;
- When dealing with conflict;
- Before you have to break the bad news to your boss, and
- After your boss yelled at you.

PROGRAMMING AND PROCESSING EMOTIONS

- When you feel sad, to find solace and be there for yourself;
- When grieving, to allow yourself a safe place to process your emotions;
- When you feel happy, to reinforce the happiness, and,
- When you feel confident, to reinforce the confidence.

I could go on forever and forever, but I think you get the idea.

Getting to Shangri-La

All the things you thought were a challenge are irrelevant.

OBSTACLES EN ROUTE TO SHANGRI-LA

Over the years, I've heard all kinds of rationalizations as to why you personally will not be able to meditate.

It's too hard.
Work is too chaotic.
I have a short attention span.
It takes years of disciplined practice to get good at it.
You have to be spiritually inclined or religious.
My mind is too busy.
I'm not that kind of person.
I can't sit still.
I have kids.
I can't sit comfortably on the floor.
I am ADD/ADHD.
I don't have time to learn how.
I don't have time to do it.
I don't have a quiet place.

If any of these things held you back in the past, then this process is for you. The technique you are about to learn bypasses all of the roadblocks above, and many others that I haven't discussed.

Even with children and a hectic work schedule, we all have the ability to take one minute.

Spirituality aside, the brain can be trained to do anything. Even with concentration challenges like ADD/ADHD you will be able to achieve this technique because it is so easy and doesn't require you to sit for extended periods of time.

Furthermore, people notice that with a bit of practice the external disturbances become a way of enhancing the inward journey.

I have yet to teach this technique to anyone who didn't choose to sit with it for longer than a minute when the time permitted because they enjoyed it so thoroughly.

PRESENTING YOUR BEST SELF

We've all had those moments when things are falling apart in our personal lives. Maybe it was a challenge with friends, family, a partner, or health. Maybe it was all of these things at the same time.

The world doesn't stop for any of us though and we still have to go in for that presentation, that interview, that exam, that family function...

I take my minute before every talk, every meeting and every client. I take my minute so that I am always presenting my best self. I take it so I am in the best possible state to deliver on what I set out for myself and those I work with. I take several minutes afterwards or longer to allow myself to process those things that are going on in my life and get back to me.

WHY DO WE NEED TO CHEAT?

To answer this we must look at the factors affecting a daily practice in traditional forms of meditation. Every single day we awake to a unique awareness of ourselves and our environment. There are many factors at play here affecting our ability to achieve the blissful brainwave frequencies of meditation. Some of these factors lie within our realm of control and influence, while others are the very reason that we seek out a practice in meditation.

The first thing to consider is the state of your **physical body**. What have you been feeding it? French fries? Salad? Steak? Were you drinking alcohol the night before or are you on a juice cleanse?

Is your body stiff, injured, supple, fit, or pregnant? All of these factors affect how you will be able to sit through a traditional meditation process (longer periods). I'm not here to tell you how to eat or look after your body, but I think we can all agree that attempting to meditate while hung over isn't going to go much better than if you were planning on running a marathon hung over. The bottom line is that what is happening with your physical body will affect your meditation practice.

Then there is your **mind**. What's happening in your world? Are your thoughts calm, clear and focused; or are you struggling to stay abreast of responsibilities at work and at home? Do you find yourself ruminating over things?

Emotionally are you happy, sad, in love, or in heartbreak?

Finally, there is your **environment**. Sometimes we might awaken to a bright and sunny day, but for some reason there's a tightness in the air and as you make your way into work you can sense that people are having road rage. Alternatively, you can have a sunny day where people are in bright cheerful moods and the world feels light. It could be rainy/cloudy and miserable or rainy/cloudy and cozy and peaceful.

As you can see, there are so many factors affecting each of us every day.

CHEATER'S ACTIVITY

Take a moment to contemplate where you are at right now.

How is your physical body feeling? How do your bones, muscles, joints, and organs feel?

What is the state of your mind like at this moment? Are your thoughts focused and concise? Are you feeling spaced out or heavy? Is there a lot of activity right now?

What is your emotional state? How do you feel right now?

What does the environment feel like around you? Does it feel like a cozy day? Is there excitement in the air? Is there a feeling of tension outside?

Finally, are all of these different factors in sync with one another?

You may wish to journal your experiences over the course of your meditation practices and noting for yourself daily what was happening with your body, your mind, your emotions and the environment.

WHEN YOU CHEAT
YOU ALWAYS WIN

With this process, you will achieve a deep state of meditation necessary for calm blissfulness every single time.

It has worked for thousands of people. It has helped with stuttering, public speaking, athletic performance, confidence and self-esteem, sleep, happiness, pain, stress and so much more.

With virtually all other forms of meditation, from day to day, you may or may not experience the deeper brainwave levels associated with advanced meditation. This technique is designed to ensure that whether you have a lighter experience or a very deep one, your brainwaves will enter into the lower healing frequencies.

Everyday you attend to your practice in a different way. Some days you may have a very deep practice and other days your meditation may be very light. While there are varying depths of trance, with the "I Cheat at Meditation" technique you will consistently enter the deeper brainwave ranges.

I know I've mentioned brainwaves and trance a few times now. Don't worry the cheat sheet is coming on that soon!

Neuroplasticity

"He who would day must first and walk and and dance; one flying."

learn to fly one
learn to stand
run and climb
cannot fly into
- Friedrich Nietzsche

noun neu·ro·plas·tic·i·ty \ ˌnu̇r-ō-pla-ˈsti-sə-tē

First known use . . . 1985
– *Merriam-Webster Dictionary, online*

. . . as the brain begins to process sensory
information, some of [its] synapses strengthen
and others weaken. Eventually, some unused
synapses are eliminated completely, a process
known as synaptic pruning, which leaves
behind efficient networks of neural connections.
Other forms of neuroplasticity operate by
much the same mechanism but under different
circumstances and sometimes only to a limited
extent. These circumstances include changes
in the body, such as the loss of a limb or sense
organ, that subsequently alter the balance
of sensory activity received by the brain. In
addition, neuroplasticity is employed by the
brain during the reinforcement of sensory
information through experience, such as in
learning and memory, and following actual
physical damage to the brain (e.g., caused by
stroke), when the brain attempts to compensate
for lost activity.
– *Encyclopedia Britannica, online*

Whether you are old or young, whether you feel old or young, whether it is an easy habit or a more challenging one, the more often you practise it, the easier it will get.

THE 'I CHEAT' DEFINITION OF NEUROPLASTICITY

Consider that the mind is plastic or like Play-Doh. It can be moulded into anything. Not only can it be moulded, it can be remoulded. If we don't like that elephant we just made, we can always knead it up and shape it into a robot. Your old habits, the ones you want to shift, are the elephant. The Play-Doh used for those old habits can be remoulded and formed to make something new such as our pathway to paradise.

We hardly ever use all of the Play-Doh and when we are done with it we put it back in its container for later. Unlike Play-Doh which dries up over time, **"Brain-Doh" never dries up. Our minds remain mouldable.** As we get older, our Brain-Doh may require a little extra kneading in the form of repetition and practice, but it never dries up.

It is said infants take 21 repetitions to learn something and completely form a new neural pathway. There is a commonly held belief that adults only need 21 days to form new habits. The truth is, and we all know this from experience, that there are habits that take a lot longer to form permanently. The older we get the more repetitions we require to do this.

We've all gone on a diet, hit the gym every morning, or read for an hour every evening for a few months or even a year. Something came up for a week, maybe you were sick or had to go on a trip, and it slipped away.

There are habits that take a commitment over time to become permanent. Since your brain is remouldable, it is important to keep active with those habits lest your brain re-distributes your Brain-Doh to the Netflix habit. I don't speak from experience here at all and I'm sure you can't relate either. (wink)

Children have it easier than us with forming new habits/moulding their Brain-Doh. You could say that their Brain-Doh is softer than ours. It is thought that this is because children spend almost all their time in the trance state. All children are in trance up to a certain age and thus they are able to form new neural pathways more easily. They also tend to feel things very deeply. The chemicals associated with feelings are pumping through their brains in higher volumes.

In the trance state we access our mind in that same way that children do. We bypass the firewall of our mind and access the spongy malleable part of it as children do. We are able to feel things more deeply and access our emotions in a more powerful way. In my professional experience, a meditative and focused state of trance allows new neural pathways to form more efficiently. This is especially noticeable in athletes who use meditation to enhance their visualization practices.

Whether you are old or young, whether you feel old or young, whether it is an easy habit or a more challenging one, the more often you practise it, the easier it will get.

This technique is designed to be as easy to do and as addictive as smoking a cigarette. Not my favourite analogy, but all of my clients who used to smoke view taking their minute of meditation as being more satisfying than any cigarette. Like smoking, it doesn't take much time and it's highly addictive. Unlike smoking, it's free and the more often you do it the healthier you become.

HOW NEUROPLASTICITY
RELATES TO CHEATING

Your mind is the rich jungle forest.

Paradise, your Shangri-La, is where you want to go.

Your 60 Second technique is the way there.

Think of the technique as a small group of hikers.

Each time you practise it you send hikers through the forest all the way to paradise.

Cheater's Tip

It's also okay to spend longer than a minute each time you practice your technique.

The first time the hikers make their way to Shangri-La, they won't make much of a disturbance in the forest. Since the forest grows back so quickly, after a few days or weeks even an experienced tracker might not be able to find traces of those hikers nor the path to Shangri-La.

Most people don't have a clearly defined path to paradise. So for them, if they find their way to paradise, the same path is not usually taken again.

The forest grows over and the search for paradise begins again.

Occasionally, a few get lucky and find paradise and manage to stay there.

Because you have this technique, the more you practise it, or rather the more hikers you send along the same path, the wider the path becomes. It starts out as a disturbance in the foliage which turns into a small trail. Eventually a path forms and soon you have your very own private speedway to paradise. Heck, you can even have your own teleport!

Since it takes only a minute and it's easy, why not take several minutes throughout the day and build your speedway faster?

Meditation
Trance
Brainwaves

Meditation is trance.

Trance is Shangri-La.

All of it is measured in brainwaves.

However you experience your light, it's all science.

A QUICKIE IN TRANCE
AKA. YOUR CHEAT SHEET ON BRAINWAVES

Before we dive into the technique, let's take a moment to look at what trance and meditation are, from a more scientific perspective.

When I use the word trance and meditation interchangeably, it's because all meditation-trance states are scientifically measurable in brainwaves.

The thing is, everyone naturally experiences all of these trance states daily. When you wake in the morning, you tend to be in that hazy part-of-me-is-still-in-bed-state (this is alpha) and for most, depending on your caffeine intake you hit beta by early to mid morning. This is where you stay until the afternoon. Depending on the intensity of your day and the quality of sleep the previous night, you may sink back into alpha if not the deeper theta range. In the early evening you rise back up to beta again and then as you fall asleep your brain moves into theta and eventually a deep delta sleep. This is the norm for most people. There are always exceptions.

There are four major categories of brainwaves: beta, alpha, theta and delta.

BETA	The alert, consciously engaged state. Logical and focused.
ALPHA	The light trance state that all children are in until the age of six. Light states of meditation & early-morning-pre-coffee-haziness.
THETA	Deep meditation begins here. Dreaming.
DELTA	Deepest known ranges of trance. Sleep & coma state here.

Be
At
The
Door

Beta
Alpha
Theta
Delta

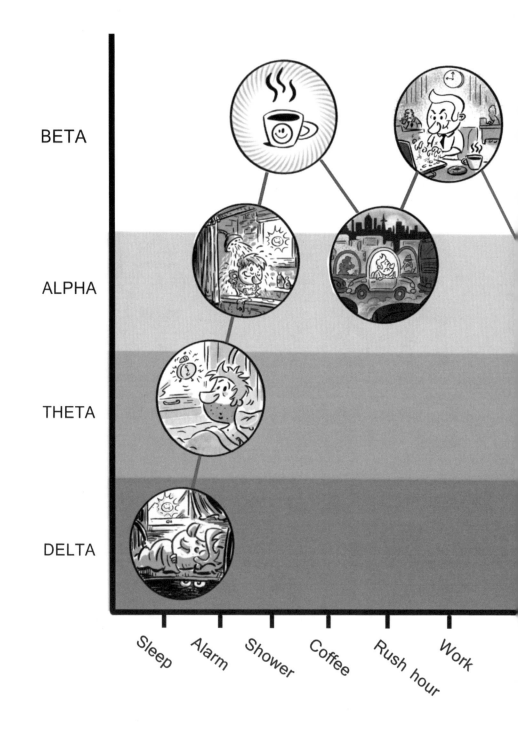

BETA

ALPHA

THETA

DELTA

Sleep Alarm Shower Coffee Rush hour Work

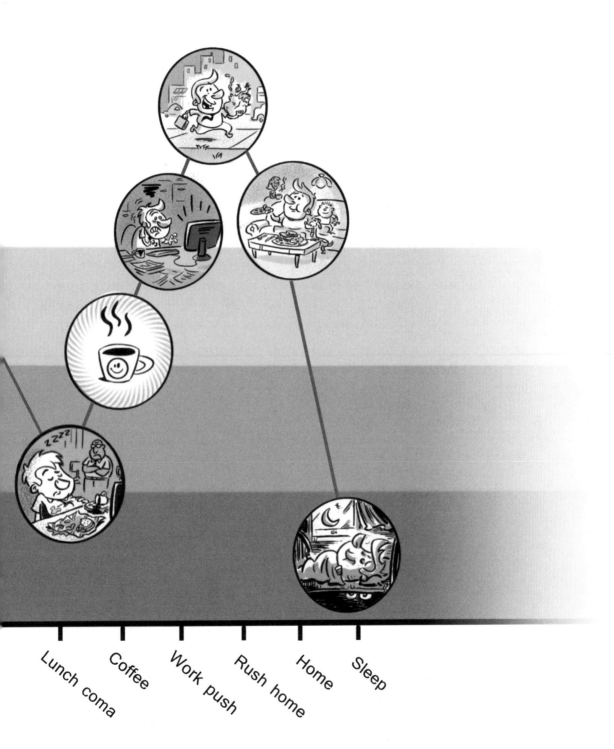

Lunch coma

Coffee

Work push

Rush home

Home

Sleep

THEORY OF MIND IN RELATION TO MEDITATION

There is a theory of mind relating to trance that I describe below.

Let's say your mind is like a brand new computer. It takes the first six to eight years of your life to load your operating system and get your basic software installed.

At six to eight years of age you begin to form a filter or firewall which finishes forming around age 14.

After this point you can install new software, but if that software is incompatible with existing software or needs updating, you need to be able to bypass the firewall. Bypassing the firewall is not so easily done.

Basically deeper brainwave levels allow us to bypass our internal firewalls making it easier for us to learn new things.

So as children we have a sponge-like ability to absorb new information and thereby create new pathways in our minds quite easily.

As adults we have that firewall that screens information before allowing it into our minds. To install or update data or remove malicious software we need to get around the firewall and the way we do that is in the trance state. That is why meditation with this technique is so powerful.

Once we have a filter, it acts to collect and hold the information we receive every day. Input that conflicts with existing programming gets filtered out of our minds regardless of its benefit.

For example:

If we don't get enough sleep or are sleeping poorly then the filter cannot clear itself out. It's similar to your computer defragmenting. We usually clear the filter and defrag the mind during REM sleep and meditative states.

Physiologically the part of the brain that is responsible for this is the Thalamus, often referred to as the gate to consciousness.

Meditation oversimplified

meditate / verb / med•i•tate /'medE,tAt/

To think deeply or focus one's mind for a period of time, in silence or with the aid of chanting for religious or spiritual purposes or as a method of relaxation.

To think deeply or calmly about something

To plan or mentally consider

Synonyms: contemplate, think, consider, muse, reflect, deliberate

– Merriam Webster Dictionary, online

FOR CHEATING'S SAKE

There are so many different kinds of meditation out there. We've looked at the traditional definition and how it's measured scientifically, but there's really no way to go into all of the different kinds of meditation and give them the respect they deserve without making volumes of books.

The process you will soon learn has a place alongside the existing meditations. Since our minds still like to categorize things, for cheating's sake, let's split all meditations into two types:

Resting & Workouts

One allows your mind to rest and regenerate; the other makes your mind work out.

THE RESTING MEDITATION

Your mind is constantly working. It is always digesting new information and sorting it out. It is continuously processing things and making choices and decisions even when you sleep.

So often we visit with our friends and while we are with them we spend that time thinking about all the things we need to get done. The call we must make, the email we have to send, that bill we need to pay. But when we go to make that call or write that email, we regretfully think about how much we wish we had enjoyed our time with our friends.

The fact is that we each have lists upon lists of things to do. Laundry, groceries, dishes, cleaning, phone calls, emails, texts, tweets, Facebook, work projects, bills, television to watch, things to learn, exercise, books to write, people to see, places to go, and things to do etc.

Tired yet? Me too.

The key word is REST.

In the resting type of meditation you allow your mind to roam freely doing whatever it wants. This freedom allows your mind to declutter or like a computer defragment in its own fluid way. Psychologists refer to this as the mind-wandering mode.

When your mind wants to wander you let it. You completely allow your mind the opportunity to decompress instead of forcing it to focus.

Types of resting meditation include free form dance (the body moves while the mind drifts), transcendental meditation, music meditations, float tanks …

Short-term objective: The resting of the mind so that it can be stronger in your daily life.

Long-term objective: The eventual stillness and bliss that happens once the mind has processed what it needs to in its own time and way.

THE WORKOUT MEDITATION

This is the type of meditation where you flex the muscle of the mind*.

Here you train your mind the way you would train your body at a gym.

You focus and re-focus. You lift the weights again and again.

Even though your mind wants to run away, you consciously and actively bring it back to the practice.

Types: Mindfulness practices, one-thought focus, chanting…

Short-term objectives: Discipline

Long-term objectives: Discipline and endurance

* While the mind is not a muscle, the analogy of it requiring practice, repetition and rest is accurate.

THE ADVANTAGES OF EACH

We all need rest between workouts. When you work out and lift weights your muscles start to get little tears.

While your mind doesn't exactly tear it still gets tired and if we look at it as though it were a muscle in the body it needs time to rest.

Believe it or not, you're working out your mind almost all the time, even when you watch television. That includes Netflix*.

The resting meditation is best when you're really busy. You don't need a workout. What you need is to rest. It is for those whose plates are excessively full and are not sleeping well. The jungle of their minds looks as though a wind storm has passed through it. What is most beneficial is an opportunity to wipe your slate clean or to clear out your filter. To reset and let all of those heavily worked muscles regenerate, heal and strengthen so that next time you can lift heavier things with greater ease, for longer periods of time. The rest allows the forest to restore itself and grow back from the devastation of the storm.

The workout meditation is best employed by those who are well rested and perhaps seeking focus. They don't necessarily have a lot on their plate and the discipline is very beneficial to forming new habits and training the brain. This would be akin to clearing new pathways in the forest.

In both cases using this technique and being in Shangri-la is going to help rest and restructure the mind. If you've noticed that I haven't written much on the workout meditation, it is only because we are constantly exercising our minds. It's rare that we don't need the rest, but when we do need to workout we need to do in a way that is steady and doesn't cause us any extra stress.

Stress triggers our adrenals, which then releases cortisol, which in turn causes weight gain in our midsections… Nobody wants that! The resting meditation actually lowers cortisol production and allows us a break. Once rested and in a resourceful state you can always work on the things you desire as you'll soon learn in Step 1 of the technique. A rested mind is one that is ready for a workout.

* Netflix has not paid me for product placement. I am open to this. Call my people.

THE BEST OF BOTH WORLDS

The beauty of the technique you are about to learn is that you'll always get the rest you need and while you are resting you can task your mind to help you with any strength training you might need. It is in the relaxed, calming state of trance that people are most able to hone and craft their best performance. A rested mind is one that is ready for a workout.

Whether you are rehearsing a speech or are a competitive athlete, the practice of visualization in the trance state can increase confidence and ease, as well as improve timing and precision.

Meditation is for everyone. Find what works for you.

Preparing to cheat at meditation

WARNING

If you're going to cheat, don't get caught.

This means no operating heavy machinery, no driving of vehicles of any kind, no bicycles (yes that is a vehicle too), no blenders, no laundry, definitely no cranes or chainsaws, no hot elements, no curling irons, no flat irons, nothing else ridiculous that you could think of doing.

And yes this does have to be written.

Two words: Darwin Awards

According to the Darwin Awards, "Natural selection deems that some individuals serve as a warning to others. Who are we to disagree? The next generation, and ever anon, is descended from the survivors."

IF YOU'RE GOING TO CHEAT, MAKE IT EASY ON YOURSELF
AKA. SETTING UP

The following setup information is important if you are planning to cheat at meditation for longer than a few minutes, like right now as you are about to listen to your audio recordings. At all times, as long as you abide by the safety regulations, anywhere goes, sitting, standing, kneeling, etc.

You wouldn't believe how many people don't make time to meditate because it's uncomfortable to sit on the floor? They think that they won't achieve enlightenment unless they're sitting on the floor with their legs crossed. They think that the pain and discomfort are something to overcome.

"It's mind over matter, and if I was really getting this whole meditation thing, I'd be able to sit cross-legged on the floor for 11 hours a day."

It's okay if you've also thought this. You're still learning how to cheat at meditation. You're not alone, when most of us think of meditation, we picture the zen master sitting on the floor in full lotus, perhaps in a diaper or saffron robes. Either way, there is a swathing of fabric in the image. There are some who think of Timothy Leary and an acid trip. But, let's get back on track.

There is something to be said for the posture and alignment of the body. Posture profoundly affects our emotional state in an instant. It affects our ability to breathe and thus the efficiency with which our mind works in meditation.

There are certain times where mind over matter applies, like when you're doing the workout-type meditation and need to focus. In these moments, being able to ignore an itch or the fly buzzing in your ear is a great thing. There is merit in being able to control oneself such that you can ignore those things.

The mind is exceptional at tuning in and out what we need to pay attention to and what we do not need to pay attention to. We do this all the time without conscious thought.

Let's regard all awareness of pain or bodily sensations as our perception of "activity in the nerves." The itch you get may be a hair tickling your face and your ability to ignore it is your success in controlling the signals your mind acknowledges. As I mentioned earlier, our minds decide what we need to pay attention to all the time.

Take for example when you get a papercut at work: at first it stings, but you're usually too busy to deal with it while you have all that work to do. You don't notice it until you're back home again and relaxing. Your mind decided what you needed to pay attention to and what you didn't. The papercut was not an imminent threat to your safety and wellbeing so your mind ignored it.

Pain is an important signal to pay attention to. While chronic pain like arthritis is something that one could train the brain to ignore, if sitting in a chair makes it easier - do it!

If you're comfortable, that's one less thing to think about.

GET SEATED

Start by finding a comfortable place to sit. I said sitting not lying down, which usually leads to sleeping instead of meditating. That's pretty much the only rule. No lying down unless you are injured or using the technique to help you fall asleep.

Sitting upright helps with not falling asleep. Ancient traditions teach that spinal alignment is integral to accessing spiritual energy and universal wisdom. Even if you're not on a spiritual quest, good posture never hurt anybody and is essential to deep breathing. Comfort is especially important for longer meditations like the first recording you will listen to.

Be kind to yourself and be comfortable. Use pillows. If you get cold, be warm and use a blanket. If it hurts to sit cross legged on the floor then "Stop it!"* Use a chair. If it hurts or you're uncomfortable, you're not going to do it. More importantly, if it hurts, don't do it.

Even when you're taking your minute, keep your spine straight and let everything else be loose so you can breathe more deeply.

I keep saying it again and again, take your minute as often as possible: Take it at your office desk. Take your minute standing while waiting in line for your latte fix. Practising in the bathroom works, too (olfactory conditions not withstanding). You can take your minute once your car is parked before you get out of it, while you're on hold, or waiting for the waiter to come. Practise at your own risk on public transit. I won't take responsibility for you missing your stop.

THE MAIN POINTS ARE:
• Be comfortable
• Be upright
• Be safe

*Credit to Bob Newhart and Saturday Night Live for this nugget of wisdom.

If you're going to cheat, make it easy on yourself. I do!

If you find it comfortable to sit on the floor. Do your best to sit with the curve in your low back (right).

If you find it difficult to keep the curve in your low back sit on a pillow, block or whatever is handy.

If you prefer to kneel, you may want to use a cushion. Whether you are sitting cross-legged, in lotus or kneeling, is it important to keep the curve (lordosis) in your low back and it is much easier to do so when your hips are higher than your knees. Since we're cheating anyways, use the pillow or cushion or block or towel or whatever helps you be more comfortable. I personally prefer to think of using props as a way of bringing the floor closer to me.

Hips higher than knees

Remember, you can sit anywhere: against a wall, in bed, on a sofa at your work desk.

Let's cheat at meditation

WARNING
AKA. THE BENEFITS

The following technique will cause a deep and lasting calmness especially with sustained exposure. Other side effects include: better sleep, improved focus and concentration, enhanced memory, genuine confidence, visible smiling, audible laughter, positivity, and physical healing.

I'LL HELP YOU CHEAT

The very first time I guide you through the steps we will take a little longer.

> Set aside 20 minutes to listen to Hiking to Zen. This would be your time to turn on the audio recording.

Make certain you will have minimal distractions. (Maybe put your phone on silent or if you are playing this from your phone, put your phone in airplane mode.) Get comfy and prepare to go into a blissful state of trance. Most importantly, don't get caught cheating!!!

Nice work! You're probably feeling very peaceful and calm. That's perfect. It's okay and completely normal if you feel like you fell asleep at points or if your mind was filled with thoughts. As long as you followed along your mind is learning how to do this technique.

Before we do this again, take a few minutes to walk, stretch, have a glass of water and use the facilities. This is going to help you learn how to go in and out of the meditative state more easily.

> This time we are going to get there faster.
> Set aside 15 minutes to listen to Strolling to Zen.

Once again, get up, shake your body out if you want to and so on.

> Time for the next one.
> Set aside five minutes to listen to Sprinting to Zen.

Notice how it gets easier and easier each time you do it? Feel free to listen to the recordings again. The more you do it, the easier it will become.

> Finally, listen to Zen in 60 Seconds.

Cheater's Audio

Go to **www.icheatatmeditation.com/member**
to get your audio

Now that you've made the journey, it's important to know that your mind will love the repetition of listening to the longer audio recording. Listen to it as often as you like. Consider it a booster to your minute technique; an extension of your time in paradise.

You have now begun to cheat at meditation. You've experienced the process. You're feeling:

CALM
CLEAR AND FOCUSED
&
ENERGIZED

You are feeling you at your best. Feel free to bask in how awesome this feels or to continue on reading. You may want to look at the Q&A section at this time (Chapter 14: The best cheaters are asking). If you're not feeling wonderful and amazing, it's probably because you didn't listen to your recording. Listen to the recordings!

It's finally time to start advancing our cheating skills!
Let's break down the steps.

The mechanics of cheating

THE MECHANICS OF CHEATING
AKA. THE STEPS

Let's break down the steps so that you can really understand how they work and refine how to do them on your own.

Follow the steps, look at the pictures and listen to the accompanying audio files.

1. SET YOUR INTENTION

2. BREATHE

3. RELEASE YOUR JAW

4. GATHER YOURSELF

5. EYE TRICK x 3

6. BLISS STATE

7. ALERT, ENERGIZED, READY

STEP 1: SET YOUR INTENTION
AKA. WHAT ARE YOU USING THIS FOR?

Why is setting an intention so important? Have you ever heard that old anecdotal saying, "never go to bed angry at your partner, or you'll wake up feeling even worse"?

There's actually something to this. We tend to encode things best when we are in that meditative trance state. Professional athletes have been using meditation and visualization for decades to enhance their ability to perform.

We actually pass through the meditative state of trance every night as we fall asleep. We've all experienced it at some point. It's that feeling you get when you know you are falling asleep and you are partially awake and partially asleep. You can sense the world around you, but you can also sense that warm welcoming sleepy oblivion. That dual awareness is measured in brainwaves very much the same way the trance state of meditation is measured. When we go to bed in a state of unresolved anger, we pass through that trance state feeling angry, the anger encodes more deeply and when we awaken we feel even worse.

People always bring up the counter-argument, "sleep on it and things will be better in the morning." Having this attitude is an intention. Not only is it an intention, it's a resourceful one. While you might be angry or perhaps even livid, you have an outlook (an intention) that things will be better. If you go to bed hoping that things will feel better in the morning, you've set your mind to work through that as you sleep. You might even have a new outlook on things in the morning.

The same is true of your minute. If you are angry at your partner, ticked off at your boss. or infuriated with your co-worker and you take your minute without setting a clear positive intention, then you could actually be strengthening the anger or whatever negative state you may be in. There are some inherent steps in the cheating process intended to overcome this like in "Step 2: The Original Cheat" that were designed to help you release things that don't serve you. But we are cheaters and thus where we can take control, avoid potential pitfalls and learn from the mistakes of others we do. On your mark, get ready, set your intention and make it count!

As we have established, intention, or desired outcome, is everything when it comes to using the meditative state of trance. Remember, setting your intention isn't about focusing on the finish line, but rather using the moment to its fullest.

At the start I recommend setting the following intentions:
  • Deep calmness;
  • Clarity and focus, and,
  • Vibrant energy.

Stick with these for at least a month or until the technique becomes a reflexive habit. It will become so easy and natural that just thinking about your practice will bring calmness, clarity and focus. Once you've practised it, you'll likely find yourself using it when you are about to open your mail, make a presentation, or engage in a challenging communication.

Have your goal, affirmation, or objective ready (deep calmness, clarity, focus, endless energy) and then close your eyes with your intention in mind.

Be clear about physical, mental, emotional and spiritual objectives. Be as precise as possible. For example:

- Physical – **Your body is at ease and your shoulders are relaxed, your arms feel heavy, your breath flows easily and deeply.**
- Mental – **Your mind is calm, clear and focused. As thoughts arise, they are released.**
- Emotional – **You feel calm, peaceful and free.**
- Spiritual – **You feel connected, intuitive and aware.**

Again, keep practising the technique with the above intentions until they feel natural. The trails in the forest of your mind (your neural pathways) need repetition to permanently form.

After that you can start setting different intentions. Whenever you set an intention, make certain each one becomes a habit before changing your intention. We will get more into setting intentions.

STEP 2: BREATHE
AKA. THE ORIGINAL CHEAT

The breath is a subconscious mechanism and a part of the autonomic nervous system and yet it is the easiest subconscious mechanism to consciously control.

Confused yet? Do you notice yourself slipping back into that peaceful state again as you read that first paragraph? This is because you've already heard it before when you listened to the recording. The pathway to paradise has already started to form.

How to use your breath to cheat:

Notice your breath. Pay attention to it. This isn't the time for heavy yogic breathing. Simply notice the natural flow of your breath. Notice how without any effort it just happens.

After a few moments, begin to inhale and exhale deeply.

Use your conscious mind to engage the creativity of your powerful subconscious to **imagine you are inhaling calmness and exhaling tension.**

Take a moment to listen to your Zen in 60 Seconds track. Close your eyes and follow along.

THE ORIGIN

Did you know that when we breath into the deeper part of our lungs we are actually getting more oxygen into our bodies? It's true. Let's take a look at the physiology of our lungs.

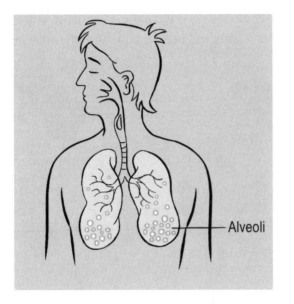

Alveoli

Cheater's Tip

A deeper breath may not actually be a bigger breath.It may be softer and lower in your body but more effective

As you can see, there are more of those dots (alveoli) towards the diaphragm at the bottom of our lungs. The alveoli in the lungs are where oxygen gets transferred into our bloodstream.

Cheater's Resource
Listen to the 3-Way Breathing Practice

STEP 2'S ANATOMY

When we breath into our shoulders we aren't accessing that alveoli-rich part of our lungs and we are actually causing our shoulders to tighten.

Notice the ease in the shoulders on the right and the raised shoulders on the left. I think it's obvious that the right is the better way to go in terms of keeping the shoulders and body feeling peaceful and calm.

Cheater's Tip

Many of you may have learned other forms of breathing (or pranayama) like ujai breathing (breathing is restricted in the throat). This is not the easiest way to release the mind or employ this technique. Allow your breath to be as natural as possible when practising Step 2.

STEP 3: JAW RELEASE
AKA. THE 'ANCIENT CHEAT'

For ages now, actors, singers and speakers have considered the release of their jaw muscles as one of the most important body parts to relax in their warm-ups. Almost all acting warm-ups include the relaxation of the jaw.

Throughout my years of meditation, the jaw has been the part of my body that would automatically release whenever I felt myself entering deep states of trance. I especially noticed this when I meditated on airplanes when I had a distinct awareness that my mouth was hanging open and people were definitely walking by ...judging...perhaps snapping a photo... in those moments, there was a part of me that felt like I ought to make the effort to close my mouth, but it felt too good.

I also noticed that every client I ever hypnotized into the deepest states of trance would naturally have a slackened jaw even if I gave no verbal cue or suggestion for their jaws to release.

Several years ago I attended a seminar on meditation led by a Sanskrit scholar, Christopher Tompkins of Harvard and Berkley.

The subject of the gathering was his translations of the ancient scriptures pertaining to meditation. It was all very fascinating if you're addicted to meditation like myself.

What was really neat was that he spoke of a something called a krama. Not karma, the stuff that goes around and later comes back to bite you in the...but krama. A krama is a sequence of yoga poses. It was said that certain kramas would lead you to enlightenment. In particular, there was one that was practised by the enlightened masters in ancient times. Throughout the scriptures, references were made to an elusive pose of enlightenment. This special pose, called the "seat of enlightenment" was considered the ultimate posture of bliss. Until recently, the description had never been found. Upon discovery of the pose and its description it seemed silly almost. Anyone who has ever experienced enlightenment or observed someone in a state of enlightenment could have described it without a second thought and definitely without decades of research. It was obvious, too easy and yet, there it was: The Seat of Enlightenment. The pose described a seated position with a straight spine, body relaxed, breath as it flows naturally, jaw relaxed and released such that lips may part or hang open, and tongue floating in the mouth.

Why is posture and the body so important? Studies show that much of one's emotional state is based on physiology. It's very difficult to feel sad when sitting upright with your shoulders back, eyes upwardly focused and a smile on your face. Similarly, it is difficult to have thoughts when your jaw is released.

Jaw relaxed   Jaw clenched

Exercise

Take a moment to sit in the described posture with your jaw released. And see if you are able to have thoughts.

Did you have thoughts? If so, your jaw probably re-engaged. If that happens, merely release it again whenever you notice it tightening or closing. There is no right or wrong here, only what is. Let what happens happen. When your jaw tightens and you notice it, release it. There is no limit on how many times this may happen. You may have days when you take your minute plus a little extra and have to re-release your jaw repeatedly and there will be days when it simply release and stays released. Go with it.

Remember, there is no right or wrong when it comes to meditating.

Every day, you will be different, your body will be different and the world around you will be different. Dedication to the practice is the practice.

It's easy to get caught up in the details, so to recap:
release the jaw, straighten the spine and relax the body.

STEP 4: GATHER YOURSELF
AKA. RECLAIM AND RESTORE YOUR ENERGY

This is one of the most empowering of all the steps, and it only takes seconds.

Why do we need to reclaim and restore our energy?

The busier we get and the more things we want to do in our lives, the more we start to fragment our mental energy towards all of these different things. We also have in our lives many "incompletes." These could be unread books, sweaters we haven't finished knitting, unfinished conversations, things from our past that we haven't resolved or let go of, ongoing projects, endless chores and errands, and much more.

These incompletes are loose ends that divert our ability to focus and be in the present. According to Daniel J. Levitin, our brains actually evolved mechanisms to help us focus and stay on top of all of these things. This area is referred to as the attentional centre of the mind (and is made up of several working parts) and it sort of juggles these to-do's around in our brains until we've taken care of them.

When we go to bed at night, instead of recapping our day, most of us are splitting our minds up towards all of the different things we have to get done in the days and weeks ahead. This doesn't exactly help us get into sleep mode anymore than it assists us in achieving a meditative state.

There are days when we leave little bits of our mental energy back in bed where we would have liked to have stayed a little longer.

Two words: snooze button.

When things pile up and we get behind, we start to leave bits of ourselves with those things so that we feel as though we are giving them the attention they deserve. We leave bits of ourselves with:

- People we are thinking about;
- Conversations we need to have or have had;
- Emails, phones, social media;
- Dirty dishes, laundry, and,
- Unread books.

In this step we take a moment to gather all of the energy from these places back into our bodies.

How do we do this?

Find a place in your body, ideally in your chest or your stomach, but perhaps that entire area of your body that you could imagine as being the area where you store your personal energy.

This does not have to be a spiritual exercise. We are using the power of our imagination, arguably one of the most powerful tools of the mind, to help ourselves get clear and focused so we can be in the present moment. Being in the present moment is a unifying element of all meditation styles and is an important component of deepening your practice. We call this place inside of yourself your centre or core.

Some people like to picture a core of energy running all the way through their body from the top of their head to the base of their spine. Others picture it in their chest or stomach. Some people picture their entire torso as being their centre. Each of us envisions this in our own way.

Energy in the chest or heart

Energy in the stomach

Energy in the entire torso

Energy from head to seat of spine

I have only one recommendation: Avoid using solely the head as your centre. This is different from the core of energy that runs from the top of the head to the seat of the spine. Although we are dealing with the mind, using the head as the spot you centre your energy in, usually lends to keeping the mind busy and active. Moving into our body (chest, stomach, trunk areas) is the most efficient way of bringing calmness to the mind.

Reclaim and restore your energy by going back to all the places you may have left your energy. Allow it to return back to your body where it belongs. You may want to imagine or envision yourself drawing your energy back into yourself with your hands. Picturing it is doing it, thinking it is doing it, pretending is doing it, imagining it is doing it, feeling it is doing it. **Imagination is how the mind works**.

This way that we have of fragmenting our energy or leaving it in places is a natural process that happens daily especially in our busy overstimulated world. Our brains actually evolved mechanisms in our prefrontal cortex that specifically work to help us remember all of these little things. This step of the technique is a way to allow that part of the mind a break, to collect ourselves, to clear away the clutter and to feel calm, centred within ourselves and energized. I want you to be able to access the full capacity of your mental energy so you have the energy to play after you've dealt with the imperatives. This means collecting yourself mentally, emotionally and spiritually (if it suits your beliefs) so that you are completely in the present moment.

Cheater's Tip

One way of decluttering a busy or noisy mind is to externalize the things in your mind. In my view there are two sides to this. The first is to get things out of your mind and the second is to have systems in place to stay organized.

I've rarely seen a highly successful person without a notebook or an app for their to-do's. They write things down, in one place. They make lists and then revise them and then make new lists. If you've ever made a list and completed the items on it, you know firsthand the gratification that comes from crossing things off.. Writing things down externalizes information and definitely makes it easier to let everything go so you don't have to worry about forgetting anything.

When thoughts seem to be bouncing around your mind, get them out in some way and create a system of remembering where to check for those things. Remembering that you need to check one list in your smart phone or one little notebook keeps things simple. It's one thing to do vs. many things.

As documented by Daniel J. Levitin in, The Organized Mind, successful people have excellent systems in place for keeping their lives organized. They hire people to do things that they are not personally required for. If someone else can do it better, they empower that person to do it for them. They tend to follow a guidelines my mentor once quaintly put as, "other people's time, other people's expertise and other people's money." Now we can't all afford a team of people executing our errands and such. You can however hire a personal organizer to help you create organizational systems and externalize your to-do's either on paper or digitally.

Picturing it is doing it.

Thinking it is doing it.

Pretending is doing it.

Imagining it is doing it.

Feeling it is doing it.

This is the nature of the way the mind works.

Use the creative power of your subconscious to your benefit. Take power over the most powerful part of your mind.

STEP 5: THE EYE TRICK
AKA. 'THE BIG CHEAT'

In this step we will be using our body's natural functions to trigger the trance state.

The most direct way to do this is by using the breath and the eyes.

Every night when we go to sleep we shift from our alert state into trance and then into sleep. By rolling your eyes up into your head, you are mimicking what they naturally do when you are about to fall asleep and thus trigger the trance state.

I'm not suggesting you try to roll your eyes up into your head so that the whites show. Think back to your childhood and your mom warning you that they might get stuck that way. Don't worry. Firstly, we are only looking up to the ceiling or towards the top of our head. Secondly, we are only straining our eyes upwards for a few seconds. Definitely not long enough for them to get stuck that way!

This trick of straining the eyes is a technique that hypnotists have been using for centuries to induce trance.

The repetition of this three times significantly deepens the trance state, taking you even deeper into your meditation.

The secret is to really let go of every physical part of your body while keeping your spine straight if possible. That means letting go of your shoulders, arms and legs as you exhale and release your gaze.

After reviewing the images, feel free to listen to your audio recording again. Rolling your eyes upwards three times isn't going to cut it. It's how you do it and the audio will help.

1)

2)

3)

Exercise

Cheaters pay attention. Can you notice the subtleties between each opening and closing of the eyes?

Begin by taking a deep breath and holding it.

Do your best to keep your shoulders at ease, but it's okay for them to be tense while you hold your breath because in a moment when you release that breath, they're going to be even more peaceful.

Remember to keep your breaths deep so we can take advantage of those alveoli (those dots). Recall the concentration of them towards the bottom of our lungs we discussed in Step 2. Oxygen is your friend.

While holding your breath open your eyes and roll them up and gaze at a point on the ceiling above you or towards your eyebrows. Move your eyes and only your eyes. Some people tend to tilt their heads up instead of moving their eyes. Hold here for 1-3 seconds.

Alternately, with your breath held, you could keep your eyes closed and roll your eyes up into your head as though you were gazing at the ceiling through the top of your head. Hold here for 1-3 seconds.

It doesn't matter whether you open or close your eyes. One is not better than the other. It's simply a matter of what you prefer.

Cheater's Tip

Skilled cheaters take a breath and look up at the ceiling simultaneously.

Exhale and release your breath and your gaze simultaneously.

Let your shoulders and arms slacken towards the floor.

If your eyes were open let your eyelids close all the way down as you release your gaze and allow every part of yourself to settle further into relaxation.

If your eyelids remained closed, as you rolled your eyes up into your head, be sure to release your gaze as you exhale.

Be sure to release the upward gaze of your eyes and your held breath at the same time.

It's important to let everything go. I know I've repeated myself several times, but it's only because I don't want your eyes to get stuck that way! Don't let mom be right.

We repeat this process two more times and what you will notice is that with each repetition you'll go deeper into calmness as the trance state deepens and the act of rolling the eyes back into the head becomes more tedious.

Cheater's Tip

Most people will feel heavier eyes as they practise this and get better at it. It's rare but some people don't physically ever feel the heaviness in their eyes. That said if you were to look at anyone's eyes during this process they would glaze over and start to redden, which are signs of entering into deeper states of trance. Don't get too ambitious. If it hurts, stop it. It is not necessary to exceed three seconds. One to two seconds is more than enough and if you hold your gaze for too long. Nobody needs an eye strain headache. As you get better and better at this you'll need less and less time in this step as your body and brain learn how to access deeper brainwaves even faster.

If it feels tedious that means you're doing it right! Even if it doesn't feel tedious, just by taking this step you will go even deeper into trance. You may or may not notice your eyes beginning to flutter. Either way, as long as you follow these steps, it will work.

Some of you will feel it right away and some of you will take a bit of practice to understand what trance feels like. It's okay.

Guess what? You've made it to Shangri-la!

STEP 6: THE BLISS STATE
AKA. SHANGRI-LA

This is where you get to insert your dreams and desires, or simply bask in the wonderful feeling of being your calmest, clearest, focused and energized best self.

It may only take a minute, but you can always stay here longer. Mind how you set up to meditate if you are planning on meditating for longer periods. (See "Setting up to cheat.")

For at least the first month your focus should be calmness, clarity and deep rest for energy. After that, see: "How to cheat at other things."

STEP 7: ALERT, ENERGIZED AND READY
AKA. THE GRACEFUL RETURN

As you get better and better at this, you will be able to go into deeper states of trance even faster. It is important to return yourself to full alertness gently. If you were deep sea diving you would return to the surface slowly and steadily. This isn't to say you need 10 minutes to come back to full alertness, but you definitely do not want to be snapping out of the trance state abruptly. I want you to feel that peacefulness and still be sharp and clear in "Beta Brainwaves" and ready to enjoy your day.

Let the following 5 steps be your guide. In time you'll develop your own way of exiting the trance state that works for you. Give yourself one to three minutes to reach full alertness until you learn how you uniquely come out of trance. There is no right or wrong. Everyone comes out at their own rate and some days may be easier than others.

HOW TO EXIT STEP BY STEP:
Notice the sounds around you.
Notice your physical relaxation.
Notice your calm clear mind.
Notice your emotions and spirit bright.
Notice your eyes bright and ready for anything.

Take a big stretch and return to whatever you were up to. Smiles and contented sighs are optional but recommended and are a common side effect of cheating.

If you're not feeling completely alert and ready for your next adventure, listen to the Extra Exit Track.

Cheater's Tip

If you do not feel fully alert, repeat the exit process with more intensity. If there is any doubt that you haven't completely come out of trance, listen to the exit track again.

Alternately or additionally drink a cool glass of water.

There is also a trick that has proven useful on a more physical level. It has been used by whirling dervishes for centuries. Understandably, after spinning for such a long time, not only have they entered into a trance, but also feel dizzy upon stopping. I don't know anyone who didn't do this as a child in the playground. Can you still remember that feeling after you stopped? Because it felt interesting, you may have let that feeling wear off slowly or you may have instinctively shaken it off physically. Here is how the dervishes do it:

Stand up and turn three times on the spot and then firmly jump three times on the spot. Next turn three times in the opposite direction and jump three times on the spot again. When jumping, use a little more force than if you were skipping with a jump rope and imagine driving yourself downwards. It may sound like I'm suggesting you do the Hokey Pokey, but it really works. The Hokey Pokey would probably work too!

 WARNING! Make sure nobody is nearby with a recording device… YouTube, Facebook, viral videos …

THE STEPS SUMMARIZED
AKA. A CHEAT SHEET

1. SET YOUR INTENTION

2. BREATHE

3. RELEASE YOUR JAW

4. GATHER YOURSELF

5. EYE TRICK x 3

6. BLISS STATE

7. ALERT, ENERGIZED, READY

Frequent dosing recommended.

10

What to expect in paradise

WHAT TO EXPECT IN PARADISE

People usually describe a deep calm that increases with practice. This is the calmness that moves through the body, the brain and the mind, the emotions and the spirit.

Each time you do it, it will get easier, but it will still vary. Day to day everything is different. Some days your filter in your mind will have a lot to declutter and there will be times when your mind is like the surface of the calmest pond. We are constantly changing and the world around us is constantly changing. Some days we feel out of sorts, and the rest of the world seems to be blissful. Other days we go out on a sunny beautiful day and there's a tightness in the air and it seems like everyone has road rage as you drive to work. There will be days when everything is in alignment and that blissful state seems to be in the air and emanating from you. Allow for these shifts and differences.

Paradise is subjective. No two people could ever really describe it the same way. No matter what your experience is from one day to the next, your practice will get you the benefits of the trance state every time. I believe this to be the best perk of being able to cheat at meditation.

WHERE AND WHEN TO CHEAT

AKA. WHEN YOU NEED IT MOST,
AND WHEN YOU DON'T

The more you do this the easier it will get. You'll get faster and faster until you won't need a full minute, but seconds. You may enjoy it so much you'll want to stay there for much longer than a minute.

Remember that repetition is everything. The more frequently you visit Shangri-La, the faster you will transform that trail in your mind into a road and into a freeway and, eventually, into a teleport.

I "cheat" at the gym, to focus my workouts; before yoga class, to get centred; before seeing clients so that I'm in the right space to greet them; before, during and after taxes so that I actually get through doing my taxes; before I write or tap into my creativity; before giving speeches.

My actors "cheat" before auditions or to get into and out of character. They use it to remember lines, they use it to get back in touch with their true self, to re-align with their purpose, to get their magic back so that they are in the zone and are tapping into their maximum magnetic force.

My athletes use it before they are about to take their swing, before a penalty shot, to heal injuries and improve response times and accuracy. To get in the zone. To sustain focus and energy.

It's okay if you get there in less than a minute

It's also okay to do it for longer and stay in the trance state longer.

When you wish to stay in the trance state for longer, it's okay to repeat the technique after a few minutes to re-deepen the trance state if you feel yourself coming out of it.

You have the recordings and can listen to them as often as you'd like. The mind loves repetition so the more you practise the better you will get at all of this.

Take less than
a minute.
Take more than a
minute.
Take a minute and
cheat at meditation
for an hour.
Just take your
minute.

How to cheat at other things

"Do, or
There is

do not. no try."

~Yoda

Star Wars: The Empire Strikes Back

SETTING INTENTIONS
AKA. AFFIRMATIONS

To establish affirmations and intentions I recommend phrasing intentions in the positive, and not the negative. It has been argued that the mind does not hear words like don't and not and that it only hears what comes before and after. Whether this is true or not, I believe in focusing on the positive. **All motivation can be simplified into two types.** We are either:

(1) **motivated to move away from negativity**
(2) **towards something pleasurable**.

Fire poker → me → moving away from fire poker = no more pain
Happier = moving towards desired outcome ← me inspired ← desire

Moving away from the negative is something people do quite naturally. This is especially true when the negative in question is palpable and or imminent. For example, smoking is neither palpable nor imminent and therefore is difficult to move away from; whereas, oncoming traffic is both imminent and palpable, so we move out of the way. It's not cheating, it's good sense. Don't get hit!

Moving towards the positive can be harder. We have a tendency to unlearn this type of motivation at a young age. Can you remember wanting to play at a friend's place or wanting a certain toy? Can you remember asking again and again and again and being answered no again and again… You cleaned your room and asked yet again. You did your chores and asked, but still you were told no. We kept on asking our parents weakening their no. We persevered until the no became a yes.

Sadly, as adults, we seemed to have lost that perseverance. Many of us have stopped asking for those things that we desire. We don't take action on our aspirations often because we are preoccupied dealing with those things that are palpable and imminent. We have learned to hear no in our minds before we have even asked. Being inspired towards the positive or for desire's sake is something that the most passionate, successful and fulfilled people practise. The leaders in our lives, the people we look up to, were the ones unwilling to take no for an answer.

I use the analogy of the fire poker because when we use a fire poker as our motivator, we can get great results under the threat of imminent pain (like the deadline you were able to meet by pulling an all-nighter). But if you keep using the fire poker, your nerve endings will eventually dull and get used to the pain. Eventually, the poker stops working. At this point, we have built a freeway to accessing that pain without even doing anything. I call this burnout.

Most of us have experienced burnout. (High-five to you if you haven't.) Either way, we have all experienced being too tired to pull that all-nighter even though the deadline was imminent. Let's face it, leaving things until the last minute isn't the best way to go about achieving your accomplishments. Doing something because you are afraid of a negative outcome isn't very much fun either.

What is healthy and most beneficial is to feel at ease when we are moving towards accomplishing things. We want to approach things in a positive steady way. We all want to be that organized person who has everything together. If you are burnt out, the fire poker isn't going to cut it. If you are not in pain, you're going to need to be inspired by something to move towards. It is the inspiration that will energize you.

I see this often with musicians I work with. "I can't write anything good because I feel no pain. I'm too happy and in love. Should I break up with him?" Beautiful things can come out of inspiration, and when one is burnt out it takes a desire that is deeply compelling to drive us towards our goals.

At any point in your life, you can have something to move towards that is positive. You may not always have something negative to move away from. There are always new dreams to be had and let's face it, the best songs were written by people who were in love.

All of this is your choice, and in my experience with my clients, focusing on moving towards the positive and what we want instead of what we don't want works best. You can always move away from the negative towards the positive, but remember that your focus is that toy that you really wanted as a child.

THE MECHANICS OF INTENTION SETTING

AKA. AFFIRMATIONS

DON'TS

So often when I work with people I ask them how they would like to feel and they respond by listing off all of the things they don't want. "I don't want to feel…and I don't want to feel…" While there is a cathartic aspect to listing your don'ts, we have already established that we want our focus on our desires.

To redirect my clients, I will repeatedly ask them how they would like to feel instead. When you start to set your own intentions, I recommend doing this yourself. Given the cathartic aspect of listing out your don'ts, feel free to get your don'ts out in writing for yourself. It can be nice to look back on where you were a week, month, or year ago and realize how your circumstances have changed for the better. If you so desire, you can be cliché about it and tear up and/or burn your old don't list.

WANTS

Next start to write out your actual wants. Get really specific here. The more specific and detailed you can be, the better your mind will accommodate your desires.

For example, if you were working on your confidence in public speaking, you wouldn't just say: "I feel confident when I speak to large or small groups."

I'll share with you what I use for speaking: "When I speak in front of groups, my voice is strong and clear. I convey my message, emotions and intentions with clarity and passion. I connect with my audience. My body is at ease and I feel strong. I am doing what I am meant to do."

NEGATIVES

If you are going to refer to a negative, the best way is to set up the negative for removal. To do this, make sure you immediately follow a negative statement with a statement of what you would like instead. For example, "I now release anger and replace it with love."

Lose the word, try. **Trying is failing with attitude.** Doing and trying both lend to your effort, but doing carries a subconscious intent towards completion; whereas, trying infers there is a possibility for failure. Why not remove all possibility of failure where you have the ability to.

LOSE THE WORD, TRY.

Also, be wary of words that include the thing that you don't want, such as non-smoker, pain-free, weight-loss … Focus instead on what is most desirable. Having a healthy and fit body, feeling strong and comfortable, feeling lighter everyday…

MAKE YOUR STATEMENTS IN THE PRESENT

Own your now. I'm not suggesting that you pretend you are 30 pounds lighter today, but that you feel lighter and lighter everyday. Instead of saying, "I will feel calm and confident," why not feel calm and confident right away. "I feel calmer and more confident with every breath I take." Inherent in this statement is the assumption that you already feel calm and confident and are building on that foundation with each day.

Avoid words like **should, would and could.** They are not in the present tense and come with a whole plethora of issues.

Use the word **I** instead of you when making reference to yourself. Own your personal statements about yourself. "When I practise my 'I Cheat at Meditation' technique, I feel calm, clear and energized."

BUILD A FUTURE CONTEXT FOR GETTING BETTER

"**Each day in every way**, I feel calmer, clearer and more focused. The **more** I practise my 'I Cheat' technique the **better** I feel."

So, please:
- **Be specific and detailed;**
- **Always replace a negative with a positive;**
- **Use "do", instead of "trying";**
- **"Don't" and "can't" are firepokers;**
- **Make "I" statements"**
- **Make statements in the present tense, and,**
- **Build a future context for getting better.**

USING THE TECHNIQUE...

TO SLEEP

This is best done right before bed to quiet your mind.

Make sure you've turned off all lights and are completely ready to go to sleep. Set your morning alarm, if you need one. Your brain will naturally switch over from the meditative trance state to a regular sleep cycle leaving you feeling refreshed and ready for an amazing day when you wake.

Sample intention: "I rest deeply and peacefully and I awake feeling refreshed and ready for an amazing day."

TO CREATE AND WRITE

Use the technique and from the meditative state, begin to write with your eyes closed.

Large sheets of paper and a pen that has a good flow help.

In this modern technological age some people like to use their computer solely, but I suggest planting some trees and opting for paper. Handwriting has a connection to the subconscious that has a way of tapping into our most creative parts. For centuries handwriting has been analyzed with incredible accuracy as a reflection of our inner natures.

Sample intention: "My mind is open and in creative flow. My mind connects easily with stimuli from outside of myself and with my unique perspective I conceive beautiful and inspiring creations."

FOR WORK-LIFE BALANCE

"I find joy in all that I do. I am focused and efficient at work and I feel grateful, free and playful when I'm with my friends and family."

FOR FITNESS

"My body is strong and receptive, all parts of me move with a fluid easy strength and I improve physically with every day."

FOR FOCUS

"My mind is clear and sharp. I find it easy and enjoyable to be completely immersed in my present task."

FOR MEMORY

"Every time I rest my mind, I strengthen it and my memory improves. I recall all that I need to with ease."

FOR GOLF

"My body is strong, open and ready. I feel my target and I am clear, focused and energized. My mind, body and will are one."

12

Cheating takes practice

Sometimes things just suck.

Such things take time to process.

It is in the moments you think you have lost everything that you realize that you always have you.

Choose and practice what you desire...

...even when things suck.

Especially when things suck.

Events pass.

Stuff goes.

You are always.

WHEN YOU DON'T FEEL LIKE DOING IT THAT'S WHEN YOU MUST DO IT

We use the technique to change the way we respond to our world. We change habits, patterns of thought, our response to things that cause us stress.

Those old habits are pathways we want to grow over in the forest within our minds. The fastest way to help them grow over is to not take those old pathways.

Consistent and frequent practice throughout our day is the best way to do this.

You're probably wondering why I keep on reiterating how important practising your technique is. I do this because it is usually in the moments when our old habits and patterns of thought creep back in, that we are least likely to want to practise our technique. It is so easy to give into what is familiar.

This is the main reason I sought to make meditation accessible throughout your day. "Zen in 60 Seconds". **Everyone can afford a minute.**

It is when those old habits are triggered that we must shift our state of being.

Those old patterns are the reason that you always start with being clear on your intention. Be in the most resourceful state you can access.

We used the breath because it is the easiest subconscious mechanism in your body you could ever bring your conscious attention to.

I tailored the technique to be so quick and easy that even when things seem most daunting, it will still be easy to do.

This may mean giving yourself a little nudge now and then.

I keep my cheat sheet on my desk next to my laptop as a reminder.

Some of my clients set an alarm (a nice one e.g. chime) to make sure they take their minute every 30 minutes or hour. Find what works for you.

My personal mantra: When I don't feel like doing it, that's when I must do it.

Practice makes permanent.

13

Cheaters are kind to themselves

"You are Everything - it's just

the sky.
else the
weather."

– Pema Chodron

shud \ shood \ verb

1. A four letter word for profanity that boxes one in with guilt, shame, expectation and other such rubbish.

shud \ noun
2. The inferior cousin of desire and choice.

– The Farzana Dictionary of Outstanding Excellence

THE "SH" WORD

Every day, every moment will be different. Remember who you are. As I always say, you are the light. You always were the light. You will always be the light. Whatever the weather may bring remember that the weather is not who you are. The things that are happening in your life are not who you really are.

One of the greatest hindrances to any process of learning or practice is restricting ourselves, or as I call like to call it, "shuding" ourselves.

"My mind shud be silent." "I shud have no thought."

This is when we think we shud be at a certain level of our meditation, or when we shud be doing something or shud be able to do something we are not currently doing.

In my vocabulary, shud was miswritten and is actually a four letter word. Where we are now is the only thing that matters. Right now is your starting point. The past is irrelevant.

> **Cheater's Tip**
>
> When you spend time trying to quiet the thoughts in your head (during your meditation), you are actually fighting the natural release of those thoughts from your mind. Say no to bullshud and allow your mind to be in whatever state it is in. The thoughts that arise, are the ones being released.

You are not your past actions. You are the choices you make today.

Just because your meditation was deep on one day, it doesn't mean it shud always be exactly the same. If you allow yourself to be free of expectations and shuds, you open yourself to being able to practise every day, all the time, whenever you need and however your meditation unfolds.

Dedication to your practice is the practice. The only shud that belongs in my world is to practise my "I Cheat" technique. More importantly, that shud is rooted in a desire, not an obligation.

Be kind to yourself and allow your experience to be whatever it is.

The best cheaters are asking...

WHEN I'M DONE CHEATING, WHERE DO I GO FROM HERE?

While there are deeper practices, start out by practising the technique for longer.

You already have details on how to get comfortable when meditating for longer periods. Make sure you have a blanket if you tend to get cold when resting for long periods of time.

Set a gentle alarm, perhaps something with gongs or chimes to bring you out of trance. Give yourself enough time to exit your meditation properly.

Additionally, you may want to seek out calming meditations that rest the mind, such as Transcendental Meditation, Sahaj Samadi or other mantra based meditations.

Perhaps you'll be inspired to go into other traditions such as Vipasana or Buddhist traditions. You may be attracted to sound and chanting or movement based styles. Whatever you choose, you always have the option of beginning with this technique and guaranteeing that you'll enter into meditative trance (in brainwaves) every single time. It only takes a few seconds. Run with it and find what works for you!

HOW DO YOU MEDITATE, FARZANA?

I am reluctant to answer this question, because I don't want to "should" you. I want your journey to be your own. All the same, this is one of the questions I am most frequently asked.

I prefer to meditate in the early morning. My preference is to meditate upon waking and/or right after some form of physical exercise.
Physical exercise works out any angst and prepares the body to sit. That said, I choose to sit in a chair.

Early morning is the quietest time in my 24-hour day. I meditate at 4a.m., partially because of how I was brought up, but also because of the natural tendency of the brain to be in the deeper theta-delta brainwave range during the early morning hours. I cheat by using my body's natural state to my advantage.

If you are going to sit for longer periods of time, initially don't worry about the when, just start. You can get into picking times later.

IS THERE A MORNING ROUTINE YOU RECOMMEND FOR MEDITATION?

Wake up. Exercise. Meditate. Eat and enjoy your day. Supplement your practice and zen state throughout the day by cheating a minute here and there.

IS IT WORKING IF MY EYELIDS FLUTTER WHEN I DO THE TECHNIQUE?

Believe it or not the fluttering of your eyelids is actually a good sign that you are entering into those deeper brainwave levels. A flutter, in other words, means that you are getting the benefits of the technique.

It is also okay if your eyelids do not flutter. Some people do and some do not experience eye flutter.

WHY DO I HAVE A SWALLOW REFLEX WHEN I DO THIS?

The reflex to swallow, dry mouth, excessive salivation or tearing of the eyes are all signs of going into a deeper trance state. When you notice these things, let them serve as a marker of your deepening state of meditation.

WHAT IF MY EYES DON'T FEEL STRAINED?

Eye strain occurs for almost all people in the muscles surrounding the eyes. That said, a small percentage of people do not experience the physical sensation of strain in and around the eyes. This is quite normal and does not affect the outcome.

WHY CAN'T I JUST ROLL MY EYES BACK THREE TIMES AND BE DONE WITH THIS TECHNIQUE?

As you already know, it's important to set your intentions before you practise the technique, so you are always taking yourself into a resourceful state. Most of all, it's how you do it not what you do. Cheating takes finesse.

WHY IS IT SO BAD TO PRACTISE THE TECHNIQUE IN A NEGATIVE STATE?

There's a phrase in the field of neuroscience that sums this up nicely. "Neurons that fire together wire together." In other words, practice makes permanent.

What you do repeatedly becomes a habit and eventually a part of who you are. Knowing this, why not always seek to reinforce the positives instead of the negatives in our life wherever possible.

WHY IS THE JAW SO IMPORTANT?

Could you not simply focus on the tips of the nostrils, or any other body part, as is done in Buddhist mindfulness meditations?

This is slightly less about anatomy and more about the purpose of why the jaw is used. The purpose is to use the physiology of the body to access the freeing state of the mind in trance. Remember that a large portion of any state we experience is physiological. It's really difficult to feel happy or resourceful if you are hunched over, breathing shallowly and looking downwards. Alternately, it is quite difficult to feel sad when you stand tall with your shoulders back and your feet planted widely and your gaze directed in front of you.

If our purpose were to train the mind to focus (work out), we could use any body part, but in this case we are resting the mind taking advantage of the fact that the mind releases thought naturally when we physically release and slacken our jaw.

WHAT IF YOU FALL ASLEEP DOING IT?

1. It was likely you needed the rest. Take your rest and meditate again when you are rested. You may need to catch up on sleep or require rest because you are going through a challenging time. Do it. Rest up. Use the powerful state of trance to assist you in getting the rest you need. While many meditators seem to do well on less sleep, there is still no replacement for good sleep to heal the body.

2. Were you lying down? It's easy to fall asleep if you were lying

down. If you were intending to use your "I Cheat" technique to create a resourceful state, then sit up and refer back to the setting-up-to-cheat chapter.

3. Be kind to yourself. If you really are sleeping every time you practise,

it might be a sign that there is something deeper going on here. Book a session with myself or one of my coaches to get to the bottom of it and always make sure there is nothing medical at play!

WHY DO I SNORE WHEN I MEDITATE? AM I ASLEEP?

It is quite common for people who snore when they sleep to snore during meditation. In the deeper states of relaxation the body mimics sleep.

While I'm not personally there to observe the difference between a deep

meditation and sleep, most people won't fall asleep in a minute or even 5-10 minutes unless they are extremely exhausted.

There are however states of meditative trance that are so deep one might

think they were asleep. Even then, there is an aspect of lucidity or a recollection of being in that deep state. For example, if you noticed you were snoring then you were not actually asleep.

CAN I PRACTISE THE TECHNIQUE BEFORE BED?

Absolutely! Refer back to how to the chapter on how to cheat at other things and stay tuned for I Cheat at Sleep.

WHY ISN'T THERE ANY MUSIC IN THE AUDIO RECORDINGS?

I specifically made certain there was no music in the recordings because you don't need music to have a great meditation.

Furthermore, I believe that as we learn, so we do. I wanted you to learn the technique in the way you would be practising it. You won't have music playing every time you take your minute. The best cheaters are the ones that can do it on their own.

DO FOOD AND DIET PLAY A ROLE?

First and foremost, what I am sharing are guidelines and by no means rules or medical advice and that where diet and nutrition are concerned, always take care of your health first and follow your health-care providers' advice.

That said, the following are a list of things that many experienced meditators and traditional lineages of meditation offer as nutritional supports to meditating.

Stay away from: Processed foods, sugars, artificial sweeteners, fried foods and meats.

It is thought in Ayurvedic traditions that pungent and strongly flavoured foods like garlic and onions can be contrary to the uplifting fruits, vegetables, nuts and seeds. That said, you couldn't possibly convince me to cut out garlic, not even on a date. It's pretty much a case of both of us having garlic, if you catch my drift.

All the same, on long retreats where you might be meditating, as I have for over 10 hours a day, the appetite does considerably drop and the need for all of that food we eat does seem to decline.

Some traditions use fasting as a form of cleansing and there are certainly studies that have indicated that the electrolytical imbalance from fasting can affect our minds. This can be seen in cultures, such as Islam where people fast from sun up to sun down during the month of Ramadan. Fasting is not however recommended for people who are pregnant or ill.

After spending some time in the Middle East during Ramadan, I personally don't recommend it for anyone planning on working a full and busy day. In those societies, the entire populace has altered work hours and breaks during the hottest parts of the day and it is understood that the ability to function at work is somewhat compromised.

Please take care of your bodies and your health and whatever people may suggest, nourish yourself!

I recommend drinking two to three litres of water a day. That's only eight to twelve, 8oz glasses of water.

At every meal let at least half of your meal be plant based. I also include chlorella and cilantro as a natural way or detoxing the body of heavy metals.

Magnesium is a favoured supplement because it soothes the nervous system and relaxes muscles in the body. It is also a major mineral in the body. It is easily obtainable at any pharmacy or health store. Follow the instructions and find the one that works best for you. Always make certain with your doctor that this is the right supplement for you.

DOES PHYSICAL FITNESS AFFECT MEDITATION?

The physical practice of yoga was originally intended to prepare the body to be able to sit in meditation for extended periods of time. Part of this was a physical preparation, but a larger part was the pacification of restlessness in the mind via physical movement. Exercise has been shown time and time again to enhance cognitive performance and support emotional stability.

IS THERE SUCH AS THING
AS TOO MUCH MEDITATION?

I believe there is. It's one thing to take your minute as many times as you need to throughout a day or to practise for long periods when on a retreat or holiday, but the general thought is 20 minutes twice a day (standard in transcendental meditation) or 15 minutes to an hour a day (in my world and other traditions).

Meditating too much can cause your mind to drift easily, making it difficult to have focus and clarity.

I say to watch out for this because, we've all met that spaced out hippie stereotype person at one point in our lives, and who wants to be that?! Granted there is potentially some chemical assistance from mother nature in that stereotype, but remember that many existing meditation traditions were not meant for householders (the every day person). Many of those existing meditations were intended for those who dedicated their life to a spiritual journey (monks, gurus etc). They had the time and it was their intention to let their minds journey away from the physical world.

WHAT IF I LIKE TO TAKE LONGER THAN
A MINUTE WHEN I CHEAT AT MEDITATION?

Cheaters don't have to follow all the rules once they have the basics down! If you want to spend more time on a particular step, go for it. It's quite normal after getting good at cheating to go into a deep trance just by noticing your breath in Step 2: Breath.

WHAT IF MY MIND WANDERS?

Let it, it is probably exactly what your mind needed.

Great minds have all required some mind wandering. Even psychologists now recognize the necessity of what is called the mind-wandering mode. In hypnotism the wandering mind is considered a way of your brain decluttering. Let it do what it needs to. Be kind to yourself.

This usually doesn't happen when you're doing the technique for a minute, but rather when we sit for longer periods of time.

Thoughts arising are not a big deal. They are a normal process of the mind venting. Let them come and go, like clouds passing in the sky.
Remember "You are the sky. Everything else - it's just the weather."
~ Pema Chodron

If you ever have any questions, you can email me at:
info@FarzanaJafferJeraj.com

Conclusion

… habit …\ˈha-bət\ … noun …

: a usual way of behaving : something that a person does often in a regular and repeated way

3. manner of conducting oneself : bearing

5. the prevailing disposition or character of a person's thoughts and feelings : mental makeup

6. a settled tendency or usual manner of behavior <her habit of taking a morning walk>

7. a : a behavior pattern acquired by frequent repetition or physiologic exposure that shows itself in regularity or increased facility of performance

b : an acquired mode of behavior that has become nearly or completely involuntary <got up early from force of habit>

– Merriam Webster Dictionary, online

WHY YOU'RE NOT REALLY CHEATING

AKA. DON'T CHEAT AT CHEATING

We've been talking about cheating, but the truth is, this isn't really a cheat. This is an efficient process designed to consistently get you into a blissful and resourceful state of trance.

Cheating in our context hasn't been about foul play or dishonesty, it's been about efficiency and learning from the successes of others rather than the error of others.

This is you actively choosing to change your brain. The fact is that it is you rewiring your brain for calmness. You are giving yourself the ability to rest your mind, restore your body and direct your focus back on to the things that matter most in your life.

Nobody really wants to be a cheater, right? While that may be debatable, it is important to know that you are actually doing the work. Every time you take your minute, you are enhancing your roadway, your neural pathway to paradise.

> It takes minutes, not a lifetime.
> Faking it is making it.
> Pretending is doing.
> Cheating is too.

I place the definition of habit because that is what I wish this to become for you. A habit is easy and can only come with practice. Remember, you still have to do the practice and practice always makes permanent.

You're not cheating, you're just getting really good at something.

ENDNOTES

Given the subjectivity of one's experience of meditation and the fact that a technique developed by a single person based on their own experiences is subjective. I was presented with the option of not having a reference section to this book.

Without conducting studies that are specifically oriented to the I Cheat at Meditation technique, I have referenced studies that support the principles of this technique scientific and otherwise. The sources cited support the ideas and thoughts expressed in the ideology of this technique. There are of course studies and sources that contradict my ideology around meditation and the mind. I am not attempting to say that this technique and everything expressed in this book is the only way to experience meditation, but that it has proven effective for myself and those with whom I have worked.

Research and studies aside, there are centuries upon centuries of "case studies" to draw wisdom from. That is to say, millions of people over the ages passed on their wisdom in the many practices of the mastery of the mind and self through meditation.

Even though, I believe everything is science, I still find the Jungian approach to be the most efficient way to study and learn about meditation. This means to understand it, we must practice it ourselves and immerse ourselves in that practice. This is of course subjective. The effectiveness of any practice is in the eye of the beholder. Be this effectiveness one of placebo or based 100% in science is yet to be determined.

Many things in this book have not been cited, sourced or referenced, as they come from my experiences and my trainings in numerous traditions. Many aspects of this technique have come from the trial and betterment through working with my clients over the years.

What I have referenced here, I have done so to respect existing lineages of meditation, but more so because I believe everything is science. More and more studies are currently being conducted on varieties of meditation and the body-mind-brain connections. This research is just the beginning.

Meditation is not merely the fluff of unicorns, fairies and angels. There is a science to it. It lives in the mechanisms of our brains and bodies and the world we live in. There is a science to everything.

Before we had science, many things seemed like magic and miracles. For centuries millions of people have had positive experiences from accessing deeper brain waves through meditation. Those people never knew brainwaves existed.

It is my wish to bring the science into meditation as much as possible, to remove the fairytale from it, but the truth is nobody truly knows what happens to each individual when they access those deeper brainwaves.

Once you are there, wherever you may go, the journey is yours.

So here they are the references for you.

NOTES

3   Maslow's Hierarchy of Needs, Original
Maslow, A. H. "A theory of human motivation." Psychological Review, no. 50 (1943): 370-396.

3   Maslow's Hierarchy of Needs,

6   I've kept the paragraphs in shortened segments for an easier read and used subheadings and lists to separate ideas.
Lujan, Heidi L., and Stephen E. DiCarlo. "First-year medical students prefer multiple learning styles." Advances in Physiology Education 30, no. 1 (2006): 13-16.

Morkes, John, and Jakob Nielsen. "Applying writing guidelines to Web pages." CHI 98 Conference Summary on Human Factors in Computing Systems (1998): 321-322.

"Teaching Strategy: Chunking." Facing History and Ourselves, accessed September 2015, www.facinghistory.org/for-educators/educator-resources/teaching-strategy/chunking

Tinker, Miles A., and Donald G. Paterson. "Studies of typographical factors influencing speed of reading. III. Length of line." Journal of Applied Psychology 13, no. 3 (1929): 205.

7   I've inserted diagrams and links to resources to supplement your experience. I've laid it out so that it is easier to digest down to how the margins have been set.

"Design for adult learning, teaching and learning theory, feedback." Michigan State University, accessed September 2015, http://learndat.tech.msu.edu/teach/teaching_styles

Goldenberg, Claude. "Instructional conversations: Promoting comprehension through discussion." The Reading Teacher (1992): 316-326.

Kumpf, Eric P. "Visual metadiscourse: Designing the considerate text." Technical Communication Quarterly 9, no. 4 (2000): 401-424.

Lujan, Heidi L., and Stephen E. DiCarlo. "First-year medical students prefer multiple learning styles." Advances in Physiology Education 30, no. 1 (2006): 13-16.

7   …fun while learning…
Agarwal, Ritu, and Elena Karahanna. "Time flies when you're having fun: Cognitive absorption and beliefs about information technology usage." Management Information Systems Quarterly (2000): 665-694.

Danckert, James A., and Ava-Ann A. Allman. "Time flies when you're having fun: Temporal estimation and the experience of boredom." Brain and Cognition 59, no. 3 (2005): 236-245.

Murden, D. "Fun aids learning, says research." Talk Business Magazine (April 15, 2014), accessed September 2015, http://talkbusinessmagazine. co.uk/2014/04/15/fun-aids-learning-research-says/

Prensky, Marc. "The motivation of gameplay: The real twenty-first century learning revolution." On the Horizon 10, no. 1 (2002): 5-11.

Southam, Marti, and Kathleen Barker Schwartz. "Laugh and learn: humor as a teaching strategy in occupational therapy education." Occupational Therapy in Health Care 18, no. 1-2 (2004): 57-70.

7   When we are having fun and laughing our brains are engaged in unique ways, we have an increased flow of neurotransmitters…
Bradshaw, Martha, and Arlene Lowenstein. Innovative Teaching Strategies in Nursing and Related Health Professions, 6th ed. Burlington: Jones & Bartlett Learning, 2013.

Johnson, Steven. Mind Wide Open: Your Brain and the Neuroscience of Everyday Life. New York: Scribner, 2004.

Scherer, Klaus R. "What are emotions? And how can they be measured?" Social Science Information 44, no. 4 (2005): 695-729.

Southam, Marti, and Kathleen Barker Schwartz. "Laugh and learn: humor as a teaching strategy in occupational therapy education." Occupational Therapy in Health Care 18, no. 1-2 (2004): 57-70.

7   Listen to the audio.
Barber, Theodore X., and Wilfried De Moor. "A theory of hypnotic induction procedures." American Journal of Clinical Hypnosis 15, no. 2 (1972): 112-135.

Lujan, Heidi L., and Stephen E. DiCarlo. "First-year medical students prefer multiple learning styles." Advances in Physiology Education 30, no. 1 (2006): 13-16.

Seitz, Aaron R., Robyn Kim, and Ladan Shams. "Sound facilitates visual learning." Current Biology 16, no. 14 (2006): 1422-1427.

Shea, Charles H., Gabriele Wulf, Jin-Hoon Park, and Briana Gaunt. "Effects of an auditory model on the learning of relative and absolute timing." Journal of Motor Behavior 33, no. 2 (2001): 127-138.

10   Cheat.
Merriam-Webster Online, s.v. "cheat," accessed September 2015, http://www.merriam-webster.com/

13   The blissfulness of meditation can be scientifically measured in brainwaves by EEG (electroencephalography).
Aftanas, L. I., and S. A. Golocheikine. "Human anterior and frontal midline theta and lower alpha reflect emotionally positive state and internalized attention: High-resolution EEG investigation of meditation." Neuroscience Letters 310, no. 1 (2001): 57-60.

Baijal, Shruti, and Narayanan Srinivasan. "Theta activity and meditative states: Spectral changes during concentrative meditation." Cognitive Processing 11, no. 1 (2010): 31-38.

Banquet, Jean-Paul. "Spectral analysis of the EEG in meditation." Electroencephalography and Clinical Neurophysiology 35, no. 2 (1973): 143-151.

Cahn, B. Rael, and John Polich. "Meditation states and traits: EEG, ERP, and neuroimaging studies." Psychological Bulletin 132, no. 2 (2006): 180.

Hebert, R., and D. Lehmann. "Theta bursts: An EEG pattern in normal subjects practising the transcendental meditation technique." Electroencephalography and Clinical Neurophysiology 42, no. 3 (1977): 397-405.

Johnston, William. Silent Music: The Science of Meditation. New York: Fordham University Press, 1997.

Lagopoulos, Jim, Jian Xu, Inge Rasmussen, Alexandra Vik, Gin S. Malhi, Carl F. Eliassen, Ingrid E. Arntsen et al. "Increased theta and alpha EEG activity during nondirective meditation." The Journal of Alternative and Complementary Medicine 15, no. 11 (2009): 1187-1192.

18   ...paradise...
Merriam-Webster Online, s.v. "paradise," accessed September 2015, http://www.merriam-webster.com/

26   It is said that the 5 people you spend the most time with are the ones you will become the most like.
Chua, Celestine. "You are the average of the five people you spend the most time with." Personal Excellence (blog), accessed September 2015, http://personalexcellence.co/blog/average-of-5-people/

Groth, Aimee. "You're the average of the five people you spend the most time with." Business Insider (July 24, 2012), accessed September 2015, http://www.businessinsider.com/jim-rohn-youre-the-average-of-the-five-people-you-spend-the-most-time-with-2012-7

26   Have you ever tried on a new habit, adopted a saying, or experimented with trying on a new disposition and after a time you realized you had done it so often it had become a part of your identity
Briñol, Pablo, Richard E. Petty, and Benjamin Wagner. "Body posture effects on self-evaluation: A self-validation approach." European Journal of Social Psychology 39, no. 6 (2009): 1053-1064.

Caspi, Avshalom, and Brent W. Roberts. "Personality Development Across the Life Course: The Argument for Change and Continuity." Psychological Inquiry 12, no. 2 (2001), 49-66.

Cherry, Kendra. "Attribution." About.com, accessed September 2015, http:// psychology.about.com/od/socialpsychology/a/attribution.htm

Craik, Fergus I.M., and Ellen Bialystok. "Cognition through the lifespan: Mechanisms of change." Trends in Cognitive Sciences 10, no. 3 (2006): 131-138.

Fournier, Gillian. "Locus of Control." PsychCentral, accessed September 2015, http://psychcentral.com/encyclopedia/2009/locus-of-control/

Vrettos, Athena. "Defining Habits: Dickens and the Psychology of Repetition." Victorian Studies 42, no. 3 (Spring 1999/2000): 399-426.

46   …neuroplasticity…
Merriam-Webster Online, s.v. "neuroplasticity," accessed September 2015, http://www.merriam-webster.com/

48   Our minds remain mouldable. As we get older, our Brain-Doh may require a little extra kneading in the form of repetition and practice, but it never dries up.

Clark, Florence, Katherine Sanders, Michael Carlson, Erna Blanche, and Jeanne Jackson. "Synthesis of habit theory." OTJR: Occupation, Participation and Health 27, no. 1 suppl (2007): 7S-23S.

Craik, Fergus I.M., and Ellen Bialystok. "Cognition through the lifespan: Mechanisms of change." Trends in Cognitive Sciences 10, no. 3 (2006): 131-138.

Gauthier, Lynne V., Edward Taub, Christi Perkins, Magdalene Ortmann, Victor W. Mark, and Gitendra Uswatte. "Remodeling the brain plastic structural brain changes produced by different motor therapies after stroke." Stroke 39, no. 5 (2008): 1520-1525.

Mundkur, Nandini. "Neuroplasticity in children." The Indian Journal of Pediatrics 72, no. 10 (2005): 855-857.

Pascual-Leone, Alvaro, Amir Amedi, Felipe Fregni, and Lotfi B. Merabet. "The plastic human brain cortex." Annual Review of Neuroscience 28 (2005): 377-401, doi:10.1146/annurev.neuro.27.070203.144216

Rossini, Paolo M., Cinzia Calautti, Flavia Pauri, and Jean-Claude Baron. "Post-stroke plastic reorganisation in the adult brain." The Lancet Neurology 2, no. 8 (2003): 493-502.

Schwartz, Jeffrey, and Rebecca Gladding. You Are Not Your Brain: The 4-Step Solution for Changing Bad Habits, Ending Unhealthy Thinking, and Taking Control of Your Life. New York: Penguin, 2011.

Zehr, Paul E. Becoming Batman: The Possibility of a Superhero. Baltimore: The Johns Hopkins University Press, 2008.

49   There is a commonly held belief that adults only need 21 days to form new habits. The truth is, and we all know this from experience, that there are habits that take a lot longer to form permanently.

Clear, James. "How long does it actually take to form a new habit? (Backed by science)." Huffington Post (April 10, 2014). Accessed September 2015, http://www.huffingtonpost.com/james-clear/forming-new-habits_b_5104807.html

Mundkur, Nandini. "Neuroplasticity in children." The Indian Journal of Pediatrics 72, no. 10 (2005): 855-857.

49   In the trance state we access our mind in that same way that children do. We bypass the firewall of our mind and access the spongy malleable part of it as children do. We are able to feel things more deeply and access our emotions in a more powerful way.

Based on the Theory of Mind as described in:

Baçar, Erol, Canan Basar-Eroglu, Sirel Karakas, and Martin Schürmann. "Gamma, alpha, delta, and theta oscillations govern cognitive processes." International Journal of Psychophysiology 39, no. 2 (2001): 241-248.

Gruzelier, John. "A theory of alpha/theta neurofeedback, creative performance enhancement, long distance functional connectivity and psychological integration." Cognitive Processing 10, no. 1 (2009): 101-109.

Kappas, John G. Professional Hypnotism Manual: Introducing Physical and Emotional Suggestibility and Sexuality. California: Panorama Publishing, 1978.

Klimesch, Wolfgang. "EEG alpha and theta oscillations reflect cognitive and memory performance: A review and analysis." Brain Research Reviews 29, no. 2 (1999): 169-195.

56   There are four major categories of brainwaves.
Barker, Wayne and Susan Burgwin. "Brain wave patterns during hypnosis, hypnotic sleep and normal sleep." Archives of Neurology and Psychiatry (1949), doi:10.1001/archneurpsyc.1949.02310160032002.

Gruzelier, John. "A theory of alpha/theta neurofeedback, creative performance enhancement, long distance functional connectivity and psychological integration." Cognitive Processing 10, no. 1 (2009): 101-109.

Klimesch, Wolfgang. "EEG alpha and theta oscillations reflect cognitive and memory performance: A review and analysis." Brain Research Reviews 29, no. 2 (1999): 169-195.

"What are brainwaves?" Brainworks, accessed September 2015, http://www.brainworksneurotherapy.com/what-are-brainwaves

"What is the function of the various brainwaves?" Scientific American (December 22, 1997), accessed September 2015, http://www.scientificamerican.com/article/what-is-the-function-of-t-1997-12-22/

56   The thing is, everyone naturally experiences all of these trance states daily.
"5 Types Of Brain Waves Frequencies: Gamma, Beta, Alpha, Theta, Delta." Mental Health Daily (blog), accessed September 2015, http://mentalhealthdaily.com/2014/04/15/5-types-of-brain-waves-frequencies-gamma-beta-alpha-theta-delta/

Frank, Gilbert, Franz Halberg, Richard Harner, James Matthews, Eugene Johnson, Howard Gravem, and Virginia Andrus. "Circadian periodicity, adrenal corticosteroids, and the EEG of normal man." Journal of Psychiatric Research 4, no. 2 (1966): 73-86.

Rodéhn Fox, Miriam. "The importance of sleep." Nursing Standard 13, no. 24 (1999): 44-47, doi:10.7748/ns1999.03.13.24.44.c7485

Strogatz, Steven H. "Norbert Wiener's Brain Waves." Frontiers in Mathematical Biology (1994): 122-138, doi:10.1007/978-3-642-50124-1_7

60   There is a theory of mind relating to trance…
Kappas, John G. Professional Hypnotism Manual: Introducing Physical and Emotional Suggestibility and Sexuality. California: Panorama Publishing, 1978.

64   …meditate…
Merriam-Webster Online, s.v. "meditate," accessed September 2015, http://www.merriam-webster.com/

66   Your mind is constantly working. It is always digesting new information and sorting it out.

Levitin, Daniel J. "Why the modern world is bad for your brain." The Guardian (January 18 2015), accessed September 2015, http://www.theguardian.com/science/2015/jan/18/modern-world-bad-for-brain-daniel-j-levitin-organized-mind-information-overload

66   The fact is that we each have lists upon lists of things to do. Laundry, groceries, dishes, cleaning, phone calls, emails, texts, tweets, Facebook, work projects, bills, television to watch, things to learn, exercise, books to write, people to see, places to go, and things to do.

Trout, J. "Differentiate or Die." Forbes (December 5, 2005), accessed September 2015, http://www.forbes.com/2005/12/02/ibm-nordstrom-cocacola-cx_jt_1205trout.html

67   The key word is REST.
Gusnard, D. A., and M.E. Raichle. "Searching for a baseline: Functional imaging and the resting human brain." Nature Reviews Neuroscience 2, no. 10 (2001): 685-694.

Raichle, M.E., A.M. MacLeod, A.Z. Snyder, J.W. Powers, D.A. Gusnard, and G.L. Shulman. "A default mode of brain function." Proceedings of the National Academy of Sciences 98, no. 2 (2001): 676-682.

67   In this type of meditation you allow your mind to roam freely… Psychologists refer to this as the mind-wandering mode.

Gusnard, D. A., and M.E. Raichle. "Searching for a baseline: Functional imaging and the resting human brain." Nature Reviews Neuroscience 2, no. 10 (2001): 685-694.

Raichle, M.E., A.M. MacLeod, A.Z. Snyder, J.W. Powers, D.A. Gusnard, and G.L. Shulman. "A default mode of brain function." Proceedings of the National Academy of Sciences 98, no. 2 (2001): 676-682.

70   The resting meditation actually lowers cortisol and allows us a break.
Green, P. "The way we live: Drowning in stuff." The New York Times (June 28, 2012).

Kirschbaum, C., O.T. Wolf, M. May, W. Wippich, and D.H. Hellhammer. "Stress- and treatment-induced elevations of cortisol levels associated with impaired declarative memory in healthy adults." Life Sciences 58, no. 17 (1996): 1475-1483

Meaney, M.J. "Increased cortisol levels and impaired cognition in humans aging: Implications for depression and dementia in later life." Review in the Neurosciences 10, no. 2 (1999): 117-140

75   Darwin Awards
The Darwin Awards yearly acknowledge people getting themselves into all manner of predicaments that could have easily been avoided with a little sense. To quote their site: "Natural selection deems that some individuals serve as a warning to others. Who are we to disagree? The next generation, ever and anon, is descended from the survivors." http://www.darwinawards.com

76   Posture profoundly affects our emotional state in an instant.
Briñol, Pablo, Richard E. Petty, and Benjamin Wagner. "Body posture effects on self-evaluation: A self-validation approach." European Journal of Social Psychology 39, no. 6 (2009): 1053-1064.

Riskind, John H., and Carolyn C. Gotay. "Physical posture: Could it have regulatory or feedback effects on motivation and emotion?" Motivation and Emotion 6, no. 3 (1982): 273-298.

Robbins, Anthony. "Master your Emotional Health and Master Your Life." The Anthony Robbins Blog, accessed September 2015, https://training.tonyrobbins.com/master-your-emotional-health-and-master-your-life/

Woolery, Alison, Hector Myers, Beth Sternlieb, and Lonnie Zeltzer. "A yoga intervention for young adults with elevated symptoms of depression." Alternative Therapies in Health and Medicine 10, no. 2 (2004): 60-63.

93   We tend to encode things best when we are in that meditative trance state. Bower, Gordon H. "Mood and memory." American Psychologist 36, no. 2 (1981): 129.

Wagstaff, Graham F., Jo Brunas-Wagstaff, Jon Cole, Luke Knapton, James Winterbottom, Vicki Crean, and Jacqueline Wheatcroft. "Facilitating memory with hypnosis, focused meditation, and eye closure." International Journal of Clinical and Experimental Hypnosis 52, no. 4 (2004): 434-455.

93   Professional athletes have been using meditation and visualization for decades to enhance their ability to perform.

Birrer, Daniel, Philipp Röthlin, and Gareth Morgan. "Mindfulness to enhance athletic performance: Theoretical considerations and possible impact mechanisms." Mindfulness 3, no. 3 (2012): 235-246.

Carlson, Caitlin. "How meditation can make you a better athlete." Shape (January 28, 2015), accessed September 2015, http://www.shape.com/lifestyle/mind-and-body/how-meditation-can-make-you-better-athlete

Janssen, Jeffrey J., and Anees A. Sheikh. "Enhancing athletic performance through imagery: An overview." In Imagery in Sports and Physical Performance, edited by A.A. Sheikh and E.R. Korn (Farmingdale: Baywood, 1994), 1-22.

Piper, Robert. "10 reasons why every athlete in the world should meditate." Huffington Post (June 15, 2013), accessed September 2015, http://www.huffingtonpost.com/robert-piper/meditation-athletes_b_3398745.html

Solberg, E. E., K. A. Berglund, O. Engen, O. Ekeberg, and M. Loeb. "The effect of meditation on shooting performance." British Journal of Sports Medicine 30, no. 4 (1996): 342-346.

Ungerleider, Steven, and Jacqueline M. Golding. "Mental practice among Olympic athletes." Perceptual and Motor Skills 72, no. 3 (1991): 1007-1017.

93   We actually pass through the meditative state of trance every night as we fall asleep

Ogilvie, Robert D. "The process of falling asleep." Sleep Medicine Reviews 5, no. 3 (2001): 247-270.

Huffman, Karen. Psychology in Action, 9th ed. New York: John Wiley & Sons, 2008.

96   Step 2: Breathe
Jerath, Ravinder and Vernon A. Barnes. "Augmentation of Mind-body Therapy and Role of Deep Slow Breathing." Journal of Complementary and Integrative Medicine 6, no. 1 (2009).

Jerath, Ravinder, John W. Edry, Vernon A. Barnes, and Vandna Jerath. "Physiology of long pranayamic breathing." Elselvier Ltd. (2006): 567-571.

97 As you can see, there are more of those dots (alveoli) towards the diaphragm at the bottom of our lungs. The alveoli in the lungs are where oxygen gets transferred into our bloodstream.

Miller-Keane Encyclopedia and Dictionary of Medicine, Nursing, and Allied Health, 7th ed., s.v. "alveoli," accessed August 24, 2015, http://medical-dictionary.thefreedictionary.com.

98   ...pranayama...
Dictionary.com, s.v. "pranayama," accessed September 2015, http://dictionary.reference.com/

98   ...ujai...
Watters, Nancy A. "Instant Stress-Buster #3: Ujai Breath." Luminous Tones (blog), accessed September 2015, http://www.luminous-tones.com/stay-tuned-blog/instant-stress-buster-3-ujai-breath

100   The Seat of Enlightenment
"Background: Christopher Tompkins." ShaivaYoga.com, accessed September 2015, http://www.shaivayoga.com/Background.html

100   Studies show that much of one's emotional state is based on physiology.Briñol, Pablo, Richard E. Petty, and Benjamin Wagner. "Body posture effects on self-evaluation: A self-validation approach." European Journal of Social Psychology 39, no. 6 (2009): 1053-1064.

Gellhorn, Ernest. "Motion and emotion: The role of proprioception in the physiology and pathology of the emotions." Psychological Review 71, no. 6 (1964): 457.

Riskind, John H., and Carolyn C. Gotay. "Physical posture: Could it have regulatory or feedback effects on motivation and emotion?" Motivation and Emotion 6, no. 3 (1982): 273-298.

Robbins, Anthony. "Master your Emotional Health and Master Your Life." The Anthony Robbins Blog, accessed September 2015, https://training.tonyrobbins.com/master-your-emotional-health-and-master-your-life/

Woolery, Alison, Hector Myers, Beth Sternlieb, and Lonnie Zeltzer. "A yoga intervention for young adults with elevated symptoms of depression." Alternative Therapies in Health and Medicine 10, no. 2 (2004): 60-63.

100   It's very difficult to feel sad easily when sitting upright with your shoulders back, eyes upwardly focused and a smile.

Briñol, Pablo, Richard E. Petty, and Benjamin Wagner. "Body posture effects on self-evaluation: A self-validation approach." European Journal of Social Psychology 39, no. 6 (2009): 1053-1064.

Gellhorn, Ernest. "Motion and emotion: The role of proprioception in the physiology and pathology of the emotions." Psychological Review 71, no. 6 (1964): 457.

"Physiological Changes Associated with Emotion." In Neuroscience, 2nd ed., edited by Dale Purves, George J. Augustine, David Fitzpatrick, Lawrence C. Katz, Anthony-Samuel LaMantia, James O. McNamara, and S. Mark Williams (Sunderland: Sinauer, 2001).

Riskind, John H., and Carolyn C. Gotay. "Physical posture: Could it have regulatory or feedback effects on motivation and emotion?" Motivation and Emotion 6, no. 3 (1982): 273-298.

Woolery, Alison, Hector Myers, Beth Sternlieb, and Lonnie Zeltzer. "A yoga intervention for young adults with elevated symptoms of depression." Alternative Therapies in Health and Medicine 10, no. 2 (2004): 60-63.

102   These incompletes are loose ends that divert our ability to focus and be in the present.

Levitin, Daniel. The Organized Mind: Thinking straight in the age of information overload. New York: Dutton, 2014.

102   Our brains actually evolved mechanisms to help us focus and stay on top of all of these things.

Levitin, Daniel. The Organized Mind: Thinking straight in the age of information overload. New York: Dutton, 2014.

107   ...externalize the things in your mind...

Levitin, Daniel. The Organized Mind: Thinking straight in the age of information overload. New York: Dutton, 2014.

107   When thoughts seem to be bouncing around your mind, get them out in some way and create a system of remembering only where to check for those things.

Levitin, Daniel. The Organized Mind: Thinking straight in the age of information overload. New York: Dutton, 2014.

107   ...successful people have excellent systems in place for keeping their lives organized.

Levitin, Daniel. The Organized Mind: Thinking straight in the age of information overload. New York: Dutton, 2014.

110   Step 5: The eye trick, AKA 'The Big Cheat'
This is based on the biology and physiology of hypnotic inductions.
References for hypnotic inductions

140   When you don't feel like doing it, that's when you must do it
Stanley, Elizabeth A., and R.A. Rensink. "Neuroplasticity, Mind Fitness, and Military Effectiveness." In Biologically-Inspired Innovation and National Security, edited by Robert E. Armstrong, Mark D. Drapeau, Cheryl A. Loeb, and James L. Valdes. (Washington: National Defense University Press, 2010), 257-279.

151   ...natural tendency of the brain to be in the deeper theta-delta brainwave range during the early morning hour.

Morse, Donald R., John S. Martin, Merrick L. Furst, and Louis L. Dubin. "A physiological and subjective evaluation of meditation, hypnosis, and relaxation." Psychosomatic Medicine 39, no. 5 (1977): 304-324.

Wallace, Robert K., and Herbert Benson. "The physiology of meditation." Scientific American 226, no. 2 (1972).

151   Believe it or not, the fluttering of your eyelids is actually a good sign that you are entering into those deeper brainwave levels.

Morse, Donald R., John S. Martin, Merrick L. Furst, and Louis L. Dubin. "A physiological and subjective evaluation of meditation, hypnosis, and relaxation." Psychosomatic Medicine 39, no. 5 (1977): 304-324.

Wallace, Robert K., and Herbert Benson. "The physiology of meditation." Scientific American 226, no. 2 (1972).

152   The purpose is to use the physiology of the body to access the freeing state of the mind in trance.

There is no scientific research I can find that suggests that morning meditation is more effective. I only have the word of millions of people over thousands of years of years suggesting that it is easy to be in the half-awake and half-asleep world when your body naturally wants to be asleep at this time and you force yourself via sitting upright to meditate. I welcome a study that examines the 4am meditator.

Stay tuned for
My Spaghetti Meditation

A Kids Guide to Getting Zen

FINDING FARZANA
OFF THE PAGE

Find out more about the book:

ICheatAtMeditation.com

Find out more about me and my other endeavours:

FarzanaJafferJeraj.com

Find me on Facebook:

Find me on Twitter: @farzanajj

Find me on Instagram: @farzanajj

My hashtags are: #ICAM #icheatatmeditation

Mo Sherwood is a television Story Artist, Illustrator cartoonist, Musician and Painter. Raised in Manitoba, he now resides and works for DreamWorks in Vancouver, British Columbia.

For more information go to MoSherwood.com